ANXIETY RESCUE

HOW TO OVERCOME ANXIETY, PANIC, AND STRESS AND RECLAIM JOY

CASSANDRA GAISFORD

A simple life, with a husband and children—a life with people you love—that is the real life.

~ Coco Chanel

PRAISE FOR ANXIETY RESCUE

"Cassandra's book is for anyone interested in ending anxiety issues, but also, for those who seek deeper meaning in their lives. *Anxiety Rescue* covers a range of healing methods and a variety of topics, from self-acceptance, to prosperity. It's a book about total well-being. Cassandra restates the wisdom of Leonardo Da Vinci, Coco Chanel and other important historical and modern-day figures who have much to teach about authenticity and success. An uplifting, informative and inspirational work! I highly recommend *Anxiety Rescue*."

~ **Valeria Teles**
Author of *Fit For Joy*

"Cassandra explores the nature of anxiety and the effect it has on our physical, emotional, and spiritual self. She draws on much of her research and writings from others of her self-help books. In true Cassandra Gaisford style of practical application—this book is for committed self-helpers."

~ **Catherine Sloan**
Counselor

"Lighthearted and uplifting! *Anxiety Rescue* is a book with a catalog of ideas, intertwined with the historical endeavors of Leonardo da Vinci and Coco Chanel. Learning about these two people while navigating how to rid my life of anxiety was fun and playful. I'm grateful to the author for taking this approach as I feel like I have a path that can easily be followed now. I highly recommend this book!"

~ **Chelsea Behrens**
Creator of *Leading with Authenticity*

*This book is dedicated to love.
And to my muses and mentors—
Leonardo da Vinci and Coco Chanel who inspire me with their resilience,
courage and fortitude…
Lorenzo, my Templar Knight,
who encourages and supports me
to make my dreams possible…
And to all my clients
who have shared their challenges with me,
and allowed me to help make their dreams come true.
Thank you
for inspiring me.*

PREFACE

"Nothing beautiful in the end comes without a measure of some pain, some frustration, some suffering."

~ His Holiness the Dalai Lama

CONTENTS

Introduction — xvii
About This Book — xxi
Author's Note — xxix

My Story — 1
1. What Is Anxiety? — 5
2. Treating Anxiety — 10
3. What Makes You Anxious? — 17
4. Anxiety For All — 20
5. How Does Anxiety Impact You? — 23
6. Your Brilliant Body—natural mood-enhancing drugs — 28

Part I
BOOK ONE: LEONARDO DA VINCI
Author's Note — 33
PRINCIPLE ONE: THE CALL FOR SUCCESS — 35
What Is Success? — 36
What Can Success Do? — 38
Success For All — 40
You're Never Too Old or Young to Make It Big — 42
Reality Check on Success — 44
Your Body Barometer — 46
Live a Significant Life — 48
Escape The Comfort Rut — 50
PRINCIPLE TWO: EMPOWER YOUR SUCCESS — 53
The Power of Passion — 54
Find Your Element — 56
Your Soul's Desire — 58
Acquire Knowledge — 60
Teach What You Want To Learn — 62
Love Fervently — 64
Understand The Rules — 66

Find Your Purpose	68
Find (And Face) Your Weakness	70
Affirm For Success	72
Be Ambitious	74
Plan For Success	76
Be Solution-Focused	78
PRINCIPLE THREE: EMPOWER YOUR VISION	81
Begin With The End in Sight	82
Journal	84
The Art Of Success	86
Brainstorm Ideas	88
Fantasia	90
Lead Don't Follow	92
Put Your Weight Into Your Dreams	94
Focus	96
Take Action	98
Ground Your Vision	100
PRINCIPLE FOUR: EMPOWER YOUR SPIRIT	103
Worship The God Within	104
Be An Outlier	107
Devote Yourself	109
Integrate Your Mind, Body and Soul	111
Work With Spirit	113
Show Up	115
Find Your Sacred Space	117
The Sacredness of Numbers	119
PRINCIPLE FIVE: EMPOWER YOUR MIND	121
Cultivate a Success Mindset	122
Motivate Yourself	124
Overcome Procrastination	126
Cultivate Hope	128
Allow No Doubt	130
Don't Let the Critics Stop You	132
Maintain Some Balance	135
Learn Your Way To Success	138
Play	140
Chase The Light	143
Learn From Failure	145

PRINCIPLE SIX: EMPOWER YOUR BODY	147
Keep Your Body Healthy	148
Stress Less	150
You Booze You Lose	152
Mindfood	154
Water Therapy	156
Move Inside Out	158
Nourish Yourself	160
Sleep Your Way To The Top	162
Plant Power	164
PRINCIPLE SEVEN: EMPOWER YOUR RELATIONSHIPS	167
Serve Only One Master	168
Fruitful Collaborations	170
Relationship Success	172
Conflict Happens	174
The Litmus Test	176
Validate Yourself	178
Social Savvy	180
Belong To Yourself	182
Balancing Responsibilites to Others	184
Stay Ahead of the Competition	186
PRINCIPLE SEVEN: EMPOWER YOUR WORK	189
Be Original	190
List Your Things To Do	192
Make Your Job Work For You	194
The Money Or Your Life	196
Steal Like An Artist	198
Step By Step	200
Do What You Are	202
Know When To Quit	204
Get Out Of Your Own Way	206
Patient Perserverance	208
Pursue Your Truth	210
Color Your Success	212
Your Beauty Spot	215
CONCLUSION	219
Conclusion: Beauty And The Best	220
The Truth About Success	223

A Few Last Words From Leonardo   227

Part II
BOOK TWO: COCO CHANEL
Author's Note   231
PRINCIPLE ONE: THE CALL FOR SUCCESS   235
What Is Success?   236
Follow Your Passion   238
Reality Check   240
Barking Up The Wrong Tree   242
Realize Your Potential   244
Live And Work With Purpose   246
PRINCIPLE TWO: EMPOWER YOUR SUCCESS   249
Dream Big   250
Perfume Your Life   253
Your Success Numbers   255
Stay Sparkly   258
Dress Joyfully   260
Keep Learning   262
PRINCIPLE THREE: EMPOWER YOUR VISION   265
Stay True To Your Vision   266
Awaken The Seer   269
Reinvent Your Life   271
Boost Your Motivation   274
Master The Elemental Art Of Simplicity   277
Make A Passion Action Plan   279
Affirm That You Deserve Success   281
PRINCIPLE FOUR: EMPOWER YOUR SPIRIT   283
Self-Reliance   284
Belong To Yourself   286
Get Creative   288
Change Your Name   291
Pray   294
Maintain Your Faith   297
Consult The Oracles   300
PRINCIPLE FIVE: EMPOWER YOUR MIND   305
Faith In Your Stars   306
Boost Your Self-Awareness   309

Create A New Life Story	312
Accent The Positive	314
Failure Is Not Fatal	316
Make Mistakes	319
Boost Your Belief	322
PRINCIPLE SIX: EMPOWER YOUR BODY	325
Sharpen Your Most Potent Tool With Scent	326
Restore Your Energy	328
Surround Yourself With Nature	331
Walk!	333
Healthy Spiritual Significance	335
Your Body Barometer	337
PRINCIPLE SEVEN: EMPOWER YOUR RELATIONSHIPS	339
Maintain Your Independence	340
Live With Others	342
Flee False Love	344
Heal Your Wounds	346
Let The Children Play	348
Conflict Happens	350
Show Your Strength	352
PRINCIPLE EIGHT: EMPOWER YOUR WORK	355
Be A Love Mark	356
Follow Your Joy	358
Do The Work	361
Take Your Chance	363
Be Original	365
Know When To Change	367
Jealous Saboteurs	369
Give Generously	372
CONCLUSION	375
Conclusion: Beauty And The Best	376
The Truth About Success	378
A Few Last Words From Coco	381
Summary of Holistic Strategies	383

EXCERPT: MID-LIFE CAREER RESCUE (EMPLOY YOURSELF)

Choose And Grow Your Own Business With Confidence	389
The Entrepreneurial Personality Quiz	393
Success Story: A Fork In the Road	397
What You've Learned So Far	409
Why Do You Want To Be Your Own Boss?	411
What You've Learned So Far	417
Pursue Your Passion Not Your Pension	419
Success Story: A Love of Good Food	427
What You've Learned So Far	433
Did you enjoy this excerpt?	437
Afterword	439
Follow Your Passion to Prosperity Online Course	442
Free Workbook!	443
Further Resources	445
Please Leave A Review	451
Blossom	453
Also by Cassandra Gaisford	455
About the Author	459
Stay In Touch	461
Acknowledgments	465
Copyright	467

INTRODUCTION

Are you feeling anxious? Despondent? Stressed or lacking energy? Sadly, you're not alone. We live in an incredibly toxic world. Anxiety, depression, and other low-vibe feelings impact so many people's mental wellbeing.

As Lady Gaga once said, "There is a lot of shame attached to mental illness, you feel like something is wrong with you…but you can't help it when in the morning you wake up, you are so tired, you are so sad, you are so full of anxiety and the shakes that you can barely think… but (opening up about mental health) was like saying this is a part of me and that's okay."

Life can be incredibly tough—more so, if you're living life raw, not dumbing or numbing your anxiety by escaping into booze, drugs or some other seemingly helpful strategy.

As you'll discover, alcohol and other forms of self-medication only make anxiety worse. Denial and dampening down feelings only deepens wounds and worries that crave to be heard, helped, and healed.

Throughout *Anxiety Rescue,* you'll find a smorgasbord of helpful,

INTRODUCTION

timely strategies. As you'll quickly discover, it's all about proactively embracing healing thoughts and healthy behaviors.

Whether it's your mind, body, or soul that needs a lift, you'll see that everything is connected. Even the darkness, despondency, and despair —the joy, the happiness, and radiant bliss.

Without darkness there would be no light. Without winter there would be no summer. Without bad times there would be no happy times. Without some anxiety you'd have nothing to warn you that you need to make a change, restore some balance, or heal a buried part of you.

Sometimes, it can be hard to delve deep or find ways to bounce back from life-sucking events and toxic people. Life can knock you around. Sometimes it can feel as though setbacks come in unrelenting waves.

You can feel like you are drowning in a sea of negativity. You can lose hope. If this feels like you, *Anxiety Rescue* comes to your aid. Developing resilience will be some of the many helpful tools you'll learn on the way.

We are not born with a fixed, unchangeable amount of resilience. It is a muscle that everyone can build, a skill anyone can master. Armed with new knowledge you can rebound from setbacks. You can learn how to find strength in the face of adversity. And you can build your courage muscles and fire up your determination to live a life of passion, love, and joy.

I'm passionate about helping people find happiness and joy. I know from experience, your health is truly where wealth lies. As a holistic therapist, I genuinely care about your health and well-being. Happier, healthier people contribute to happier, healthier communities.

I hope this book provides some helpful insights and strategies to help you flourish in the wake of any current and future demands you may be experiencing.

You'll find strategies that I've used successfully, personally and professionally to end anxiety, manage stress, and find strength in the face of calamity.

What would Leonardo da Vinci or Coco Chanel do?

Everyday problems solved by history's most remarkable men and women.

One of my favorite strategies is looking at the success and wellbeing strategies of people I admire. Success and happiness is living life on your terms and no one knows this better than the ultimate freedom-fighters Leonardo da Vinci and Coco Chanel.

That's why *Anxiety Rescue* offers fresh, fun—and scientifically validated—easy to follow, and simple actionable steps to help you tame anxiety, manage stress, overcome depression, change careers, improve your relationships—and more.

Before we continue, there's just one thing you need to know about this book.

ABOUT THIS BOOK

*Anxiety Rescu*e offers a progressive program of holistic—mental, emotional, physical and spiritual—study, guiding you through essential concepts, themes, and practices on the path to well-being, joy, and happiness.

For many people, the approach is nothing less than transformational. More than a collection of thoughts for the day,

Why I wrote this book

I'm a New Zealand trained and qualified holistic therapist. Throughout my counseling and psychology studies, I was so disillusioned and disappointed by the emphasis given to disease and pathologizing those with mental 'illness'.

Frustrated and craving new solutions, I drew my inspiration from the work of leading Māori health advocate and researcher Professor Sir Mason Durie.

Durie created a health and wellness model known as to *Te Whare Tapa Whā*. *Whare*, in Māori, means home, and with its four pillars of health, Durie's model emphasizes the importance of an integrated approach to health and wellbeing.

Twenty or so years ago talk of holistic health, especially those that integrated spiritual aspects to healing, was considered akin to witchcraft, and certainly not treated seriously. I'm heartened to see conventional practitioners have caught up with what many indigenous people have long known to be true.

Thinking of health as a home is a beautiful way to come back to yourself. To come home—where your heart is. Where you feel safe.

The whare, known as Te Whare Tapa Whā, has four walls and each wall represents a different dimension of health.

These four pillars are:

- **Taha tinana (physical health)**
- **Taha wairua (spiritual health)**
- **Taha whānau (family health)**
- **Taha hinengaro (mental & Emotional health)**

With its strong foundations and four equal sides, it powerfully and simply illustrates the four dimensions of wellbeing that are core to the tools I share throughout *Anxiety Rescue*.

Should one of the four dimensions be missing, neglected, or in some way damaged, a person, or a community, may become 'unbalanced' and subsequently unwell. No doubt you've experienced this yourself—either within your own 'home' or within the larger, extended home of our communities and the world at large.

We know that 40 million people over the age of 18 suffer from anxiety disorders in the United States alone. That statistic alone tells you something is seriously out of balance.

Interestingly, many of my anxious, stressed, or depressed clients who come to counseling or coaching session tell me that one of the things they'd most like to achieve is balance. Yet, in almost all cases they don't know what that means or looks like, or in what areas they are out of balance.

All too often, their nutrition is woeful and exercise seriously lacking (physical health). Similarly, the spiritual dimension is largely neglected or totally ignored. Thoughts and emotions, riddled with stress and anxiety, skew downwards, and relationships are under duress.

Happily, where there's a problem, there's a cure. Worryingly, some statistics suggest only 36.9% of those suffering seek treatment even though anxiety is highly treatable—naturally.

THE EIGHT PRINCIPLES OF SUCCESS

Leonardo da Vinci was a systems thinker who recognized and valued the interconnectedness of everything. He can teach us many lessons, including the link between passion and inspiration, mental strength, emotional resilience, spiritual power, health, and well-being, empowering relationships, smart goals and authentic success.

I've sectioned *Anxiety Rescue* into a cluster of principles. Principles aren't constricting rules unable to be shaped, but general and fundamental truths which may be used to help guide your health, wellbeing and lifestyle choices.

Expanding upon Te Whare Tapa Whā, Anxiety Rescue takes a broader look at what it means, and what it takes, to be successful. Work-related anxiety is a major source of stress—one, along with other triggers, we will address within this book.

The quest for success, as you'll discover, can trigger many people's stress and anxiety. However, too often we think too narrowly, or not at all, about what really matters—which is why I'm placing success center stage throughout *Anxiety Res*cue.

Success includes maintaining good health, energy, and enthusiasm for life, fulfilling relationships, creative freedom, well-being, peace of mind, happiness and joy. Success also includes the ability to achieve your desires—whatever these may be.

Let's look briefly at The Eight Principles of Success and what each will cover:

Principle One, "The Call For Success" will help you explore the truth about success and define success on your own terms. You'll discover the rewards and 'realities' of success, and intensify success-building beliefs.

Principle Two, "Empower Your Success," will help you learn why igniting the fire within, love, and heeding the call for passion is the cornerstone of future success. You'll clarify who you really are and who you want to be, discover your elemental, signature strengths, and clarify your passion criteria.

Sight was the sense Leonardo and Coco valued above all else. **Principle Three, "Empower Your Vision,"** will help you clarify and visualize what you really want to achieve. You'll then be better able to decide where best to invest your time and energy. You'll also begin exploring ways to develop your life and career in light of your passions and life purpose, maintain focus and bring your vision into successful reality.

Principle Four, "Empower Your Spirit," urges you to pay attention to the things that feed your soul, awaken your curiosity, stir your imagination and create passion in your life.

Principle Five, "Empower Your Mind," looks at ways to cultivate a success mindset. You'll also identify strategies to overcome obstacles and to maximize your success, and ways to work less but achieve more to gain greater balance and fulfillment.

Your health is your wealth yet it's often a neglected part of success. **Principle Six, "Empower Your Body,"** recognizes the importance of a strong, flexible and healthy body to your mental, emotional, physical and spiritual success.

You'll be reminded of simple strategies which reinforce the importance of quality of breath, movement, nutrition, and sleep. Avoiding burnout is also a huge factor in attaining and sustaining success. When you do less and look after yourself more, you can and will achieve success.

Principle Seven, "Empower Your Relationships" will help you boost your awareness of how surrounding yourself with your vibe tribe will fast-track your success, and when it's best to go it alone.

Anxiety Rescue ends with **Principle Eight, "Empower Your Work"** emphasizes the role of authenticity and being who you are. You'll also learn how to 'fake it until you make it' and be inspired by others success. Importantly you'll learn how following your own truth will set you free.

HOW TO BEST ENJOY THIS BOOK

Think of *Anxiety Rescue* like a shot of espresso. Sometimes one quick hit is all it takes to get started. Sometimes you need a few shots to sustain your energy. Or maybe you need a bigger motivational hit and then you're on your way.

You're in control of what works best for you. Go at your own pace, but resist over-caffeinating. A little bit of guidance here-and-there can do as much to fast-track your success, as consuming all the principles in one hit.

Skim to sections that are most relevant to you, and return to familiar ground to reinforce home-truths. But most of all enjoy your experience.

LESS IS MORE

If you've recently picked up this book the chances are you're feeling anxious and perhaps overwhelmed. If you're like me, and many of my clients, less really is more when it comes to digesting information—no matter how beneficial.

For this reason, I've created *Anxiety Rescue* as a two-part book. Each book stands alone and shares the anxiety rescue strategies of Leonardo da Vinci and Coco Chanel—and many other successful artists, business people, and inspiring personalities.

As Buddha once said, "There is a most wonderful way to help living beings overcome grief and sorrow, end pain and anxiety, and realize the highest happiness. That way is the establishment of mindfulness."

Each book in the *Anxiety Rescue* series will help you mind your way to health—naturally and holistically.

This may be a little book, but the concrete steps and practical tools I share in these pages are powerful solutions regardless of your goals, profession, skills, experience, age, and current situation.

They're a seamless blend of ancient wisdom and modern science. They are timeless and limitless, so it's never "too late" or "too soon" to bounce away from anxiety and despair towards great freedom and joy.

Anxiety Rescue offers short, sound-bites of stand-alone readings designed to help you cultivate resilience and awareness amid the challenges of daily living.

More than a collection of thoughts for the day, *Anxiety Rescue* offers a progressive program of holistic—mental, emotional, physical and spiritual—study, guiding you through essential concepts, themes, and practices on the path to well-being, joy, and happiness.

The teachings are gently humorous, sometimes challenging, occasionally provocative, but always compassionate and kind, and, I hope, seemingly infinitely wise—and easy to apply

All that I share are strategies that have worked for me personally through many of my own life challenges, and for my clients in my professional work as a holistic therapist, counselor, and empowerment coach.

Anxiety Rescue features the most essential and stirring passages from my previous books, exploring topics such as: meditation, mindfulness, positive health behaviors, and working with fear, depression, anxiety, and other painful emotions. *Anxiety Rescue* expands upon my previous books in that it encourages a more playful approach to the seriousness of life and the ever-present stressors we all face.

Through the course of this book, you will learn practical, creative and simple methods for heightening awareness and overcoming habitual patterns that block happiness and joy and hold you back.

My hope is that next time you are faced with a setback or adversity, one simple phrase will come to mind: "Love what arises." And then, having been reminded that bouncing back from setbacks in an accepting and loving manner is the test of your power, that you will then go quickly into resilience mode and apply the strategies you have learned in this book.

If when next faced with a challenge, your default thoughts are 'allow', and 'how can I love what shows up?' then I will consider this book a success.

HOW TO USE THIS BOOK

There is no 'right' or 'wrong' way to work with *Anxiety Rescue*. It's a very flexible tool—the only requirement is that you use it in a way that meets your needs. For example, you may wish to work through the book and exercises sequentially. Alternatively, you may wish to work intuitively and complete the exercises in an ad hoc fashion. Or just start where you need to start.

Each chapter can be read independently. You may wish to read a chapter each week, fortnight or month. Or you may wish to use your intuition and select a page at random, or simply follow your curiosity.

Web links throughout the book and the supplementary resources will help encourage further moments of insight, inspiration, and clarity about the anxiety cure that's right for you.

Extra Support: Anxiety Rescue Companion Workbook

Anxiety Rescue (the book) offers you information about overcoming anxiety, building resilience and finding joy. Reading a book is great but applying the teachings and writing things down in a dedicated space helps bring the learning alive, deepens your self-awareness, and enables you to make real-world change. Reading gives you knowledge, but reflecting upon and applying that knowledge creates true empowerment.

By writing and recording your responses you're rewriting the story of your life. As Seth Godin states, "Here's the thing: The book that will most change your life is the book you write. The act of writing things down, of justifying your actions, of being cogent and clear, and forthright—that's how you change."

The Anxiety Rescue Companion Workbook will support you through the learning and show you how to create real and meaningful change in your life...simply and joyfully.

So… are you ready? Are you ready to dramatically improve your happiness, success and personal fulfillment? If you've come this far, I think you are…

Let's get going…

AUTHOR'S NOTE

It always really touches me when I realize that what I do has an impact on people. We've all been through tough situations. Not many of us escape childhood unscathed. Few of us survive working life or relationships without scars. I work from that experience. If what I say, write, or do inspires people or gives them strength, courage, or hope, I'm over the moon.

Like many of my books, I write to inspire myself. I take issues I am struggling with, or new learnings that have deeply impacted me, and share them in my books.

Anxiety Rescue is one of these books. I'm tempted to say that it's a concise guide to overcoming anxiety and making the most of your life. It is. And it isn't.

As I wrote this book, so many factors which impact anxiety came to light. Many of them are ignored by general practitioners and doctors —the very people many of us go when we're feeling stressed, anxious, or just plain unwell. Some, are viewed skeptically by psychologists and psychiatrists.

Yet times are changing, the old ways aren't working. Prescription medication and pharmaceutical drugs are being consumed in exploding quantities, and still, anxiety rates and other mental illnesses are still soaring.

Increasingly science is validating what ancient wisdom has been telling us for years. You only have to consider how main-stream meditation, yoga, acupressure, and other holistic therapies have become, to witness the emergence.

Anxiety Rescue is based on clinically-proven techniques and integrates modern science with other healing modalities.

From my own professional and personal experience, I know we can heal ourselves. A great deal many people don't need pills to feel calm, happy, healthy, and inspired. Some do.

I am not against prescription drugs, but what concerns me, as it may you, is that many anxious, stressed, and depressed people are not offered a choice. Nor do they benefit from someone taking an inventory of their life and analyzing the traumatic events or stressors that may be impacting their anxiety levels.

Like Len, who, aged 42-year-old man who had suffered work-related burnout, and sought relief from his doctor. He was, quite rightly, alarmed that his doctor told him that the only cure was medication. He left his doctor's office empty-handed.

Ten years later, a diagnosis of complex trauma, not only made sense but also provided a roadmap to lasting healing. I'll be sharing more of his story in a book I plan to write called, Leaving Jehovah—Surviving the Cult of Toxic Control and Shame.

Or, Sarah, who'd been taking anti-depressants for years but had noticed her anxiety rates returning and no longer wanted to be on medication. Counseling and engaging in talk-therapy gave a voice to wounds she had repressed. When darkness was brought to light, and armed with new tools of self-care, including meditation and nutrition, her anxiety rates disappeared.

I'm not bagging medication. Not by any means. My purpose in

writing *Anxiety Rescue* is to share alternative routes to healing—lasting ones that enable you to be empowered and chose the best course of action for you.

No two people are the same. We have not had the same childhoods, the same school experiences, or workplace trauma. I speak from my own experience—both what has worked for me, and what has worked for my clients.

With over twenty-five years of expertise working in therapeutic professions, most lately as a child therapist and relationship counselor, I know what works.

As you'll read in the chapter, "My Story," I've swum through a tsunami of trauma, hurts, and humiliations and drawn on a range of modalities to help me not just survive, but also thrive.

My hope is in reading this book, you will emerge stronger, happier, healthier, and more thankful too.

A large part of my healing has involved following my joy—something you'll learn to discover for yourself in this book.

I use my passion journal to visualize, gain clarity, and create my preferred future—including my health goals. My clients find this works for them too—along with the other strategies I share in *Anxiety Rescue*.

In this era of anxiety and distraction, the need for simple, life-affirming, health-enhancing messages is even more important. If you are looking for inspiration and practical tips, in short, sweet sound bites, this guide is for you.

Similarly, if you are a grazer, or someone more methodical, this guide will also work for you. Pick a page at random, or work through the four pillars of health sequentially.

I encourage you to experiment, be open-minded and try new things. I promise you will achieve outstanding results.

Let experience be your guide, as it has been mine. Give your brain a well-needed break. Let go of 'why', and embrace how you *feel*, or how you want to feel. Honor the messages from your intuition and follow your path with heart.

Laura, who at one stage seemed rudderless career-wise, did just that. Workplace stress was a major source of her anxiety. Finding her passion and following her joy sparked a determination to start her own business. She felt the fear and went for it anyway, emboldened by a desire to live and work like those she looked up to. It was that simple.

As with all of my books, many of the examples I share were inspired by true events in my own life. At the time of writing, I recalled one of the first times I trusted the spiritual realm. I was a teenager when my paternal grandmother was channeled by a psychic and my disbelieving and skeptical self was asked, "Your grandmother says you don't believe she is here. But she is holding out a flower, and she is asking, 'Do you remember the jasmine flowers growing over the house?'

I didn't.

But when I drove home I called into to Araby Lodge, where my grandmother used to live, and where until her death, she bred and trained her beloved horses. At the time my father lived in her house. I asked him, "What is that vine growing over the house?"

I didn't want to tell him anything about what the psychic had said because I was still skeptical and I didn't want to influence the answer. My father said, "Oh, that old jasmine vine? That's been there forever."

My heart nearly leaped out of my chest. It was at that point that I began to believe in spiritual and psychic phenomena, and in time, many years later, to awaken my own gifts. These gifts weren't awakened without considerable anxiety—something I talk more about in the chapter, "Shadow Work."

It's a timely reminder of just how far following my passion and being free to be me has taken me—the shy girl who was once afraid of being seen and was terrified of her ability to channel.

As I share in many of my books I hope the following quote is as apt for you as it was for me:

"Your staying in the shadows doesn't serve the world."

Here's to learning from our anxiety and transforming our lives with passion, joy, and purpose!

MY STORY

I've experienced some horror work experiences during my life and career—everything from toxic shaming, acute bullying, and being physically threatened. As recently as last year, I experienced the ruthless, underhand, malicious tactics of a narcissistic woman who tried to destroy my career.

Unsurprisingly, all of these experience increased my anxiety levels. Had I not trained to be a therapist and invested so much time and energy in self-care and resilience strategies I'm not sure I could have coped. Many of these strategies, and those that have helped my clients, I share in the pages that follow.

For most of my childhood, and well into my adulthood, I suffered from what I now know was social anxiety. For many, many years it remained undiagnosed and untreated. Were it not for the wise counsel of a psychic when I was in my teens who encouraged me to turn my wounds into healing by training to become a counselor, I may still be suffering silently. Yes, folks, there is such a thing as the 'helpers high.' Helping others feels good.

The source of my anxiety can be attributed in part to narcissistic abuse and toxic shaming. Some healers have attributed it to a past-life trauma that I carried forward into this life. They told me that I walk the path of jealousy and that relationships are my greatest challenges, but also my most powerful avenue of healing.

You may not believe in past lives or reincarnation and you do not need to in order to benefit from the help contained within this book and others in the *Anxiety Rescue* series.

But, in the spirit of authenticity, it feels important to share how I have experienced much healing by journeying into the mystery of mysteries —both the body's and the soul's journey. It is for this reason, amongst others that I have devoted a whole section to spiritual health.

I learned later in life, and continue to learn, that healing my family trauma and helping others is my soul purpose in this lifetime.

My purpose can be summed up in one word—love.

To help others love and be loved in return, including self-love and valuing ourselves more than the poisons we may have ingested from people, experiences, circumstances, as we go through this lifetime, is a great joy.

However, it took me many years to find the gift of my anxiety. My hope is that by writing *Anxiety Rescue*, I may speed up this journey for you.

My anxiety was so bad for most of my teens I tried to drink my way to confidence and numb my anxious feelings with alcohol. In fact, for many years I was so acutely self-conscious I wore green foundation under my makeup to try to hide my blushing face.

People used to call me 'beetroot' and laugh at me. I was also mercilessly body shamed during my childhood and teenage years. Honestly, for so much of my life all I wanted to do was hide. Often I didn't care if I lived or died.

Anxiety will do that to you—until you befriend it and learn what it wants you to know.

When I was planning my wedding in my late twenties, I wanted a table down the back where no one could see me. Have you ever been to a wedding where the bride wanted to hide?

That's why, untreated, anxiety is so cruel. It can make us want to stay in the shadows. It can prevent us from standing in the light. Anxiety left unchallenged can deny us from acknowledging our gifts. It can also leave us splintered, in denial or fear or shame, of those aspects of our personality we need to wield from time to time—but have been taught to devalue and deny.

Saying no to denying who we really are and who we truly want to be and showing up, warts and all reduces anxiety. Self-acceptance and integration of the polarities within us—the light and the dark, the fear and the courage, the sadness, and the anger, the anger and the joy, and the other dualities that, unless befriended wage war within, is the road to inner peace.

We'll dive deeper into the value of integrating shadow work in *Anxiety Rescue*.

For many years I didn't live authentically. I tried, somewhat unsuccessfully, to be someone else. I tried to be who others wanted me to be. Sometimes this was an act of self-preservation driven by fear. Often it was a mistaken belief about my value and the value of my gifts.

As I've shared in many of my other self-empowerment books, I was once told that I had the soul of an artist. Actively discouraged in childhood, for a long time I'd closed off that side of me. I began my career as a bank teller, then as an accountant, then as a recruitment consultant, followed by more 'business-minded' careers.

Each time I went further and further away from who I truly was and the things that gave me joy.

As you'll discover in *Anxiety Rescue*, reclaiming joy and living on purpose is a powerful antidote for anxiety. It offers holistic, integrated healing on so many levels—mind, body, and soul.

Recently, in my early fifties, I was been diagnosed with generalized trauma. All I can say is "Wow! What a relief!

No wonder life has felt such a struggle,

Generalized trauma is similar to Post Traumatic Stress Disorder, except that rather than being caused by one traumatic event, it covers a multitude of traumatic events.

Essentially, as Dr. Diane Langberg, Clinical Psychologist and Co-Leader of the Global Trauma Recovery Institute, says if you suffer generalized trauma you've effectively been marinated in trauma from an early age.

Talk about toxicity in the body.

I count myself lucky. Which may surprise you. But as you'll discover in *Anxiety Rescue,* when we befriend our anxiety we can find great fulfillment, purpose, and joy.

As the Persian poet and philosopher Rumi once said, "Our wounds are where the light comes in."

Light, love, kindness, hope—these positive energies provide the healing balm we all need.

My trauma, my anxiety, and my depression have led me to my Dharma or my purpose in life. My hope is that all that I share in *Anxiety Rescue* will help you too.

Much love to you

1

WHAT IS ANXIETY?

Anxiety can feel like cancer—all invasive and equally as toxic. But it's not cancer. You can't cut it out, section it, or annihilate with chemical warfare. Anxiety is a feeling. It's got plenty to say and very often a lot to teach you.

You can ignore it, befriend it, or tackle it—but you can't repress it. Not for long. Somewhere, somehow your body keeps the score. The best approach is a multifaceted one, as you will discover, in *Anxiety Rescue*.

Shame, guilt, blame, loss, grief, privilege, insecurity, addiction, identity, love—anxiety feeds off them all. Anxiety is part of being human. It tells us we're still standing. It tells us we're still alive.

But too much anxiety, like too much of anything, is toxic to our mind, body, and soul.

WHAT IS ANXIETY?

Definitions of anxiety vary. Anxiety to me is a crawling, ever-circling predator that feeds on fear and devours the things I love. It's an overwhelming feeling of worry and sense of dread that can spiral out of control sometimes. Which is why I put a lot of time and energy into self-care.

Anxiety is the big brother of stress, toxic stress. It's good to know this because, as you'll discover proactively managing your stress levels and engaging in activities that increase resilience can help you tame this bully easily.

Most of us feel worried at some point in our lives and experience situations that can cause us to feel anxious. While the 'right' amount of anxiety can help us perform better and stimulate action, too much anxiety can tip things out of balance.

Feelings of worry or anxiety are part of a healthy emotional experience. Feeling anxious can warn you and urge you to take care. But when it comes to an intense, prolonged experience, anxiety can be excruciating, unbearable and even debilitating.

In the absence of panic attacks, we may think we are just worrying too much. Our struggles of constant worry may be ignored, minimized or dismissed and, in turn, not properly diagnosed, healed or treated. This is also the case for those with undiagnosed trauma.

You may be surprised to learn how dismissing the impact of traumatic events is negatively impacting your anxiety. You may feel as I once did those things that have happened to you are, "normal" and "just a fact of life." You may be heartened to discover that in no way has your life been normal. Sometimes unearthing the truth provides tremendous clarity and healing. It did for me. It will for you.

In 2018, Actress Glenn Close revealed how her childhood gave her "a kind of Post Traumatic Stress Disorder (PSTD)." Only in her sixties did she seek help to heal the emotional trauma of being raised within a right-wing religious cult for thirteen years when she was just seven.

"I visited a childhood trauma specialist not too long ago—even at my age which is kind of astounding. But it establishes these trigger points that affect you for the rest of your life," Close revealed in an interview in 2018.

"I think anybody who has gone through any kind of experience like that doesn't want to be affected by it. I think it really is interesting how deep it runs," she said.

Similarly, a client of mine who had suffered childhood sexual abuse as a young boy, waited forty years before seeking therapy. He felt so liberated finally purging those wounds and regaining his life.

SYMPTOMS

Anxiety can quickly spiral out of control and contribute to a range of mental health challenges. The primary source used to classify mental illnesses is provided by the American Psychiatric Association and their Diagnostic and Statistical Manual of Mental Disorders known as the DSM.

Professionals referring to the DSM look for factors like excessive, hindering worry paired with a variety of physical symptoms, then use assessments to make a diagnosis, and rule out other possibilities.

The DSM-5, for example, outlines specific criteria, or symptoms, to help professionals diagnose generalized anxiety disorder (GAD) and, in turn, create a more effective plan of care. While some professionals may prescribe medication, as you'll discover in this book, this is not the only, nor always, effective way to treat anxiety.

When assessing for GAD, clinical professionals are looking for the following:

1. The presence of excessive anxiety and worry about a variety of topics, events, or activities. Worry occurs more often than not for at least 6 months and is clearly excessive.
2. The worry is experienced as very challenging to control. The worry in both adults and children may easily shift from one topic to another.
3. The anxiety and worry are accompanied with at least three of the following physical or cognitive symptoms (In children, only one symptom is necessary for a diagnosis of GAD):

- Edginess or restlessness
- Tiring easily; more fatigued than usual
- Impaired concentration or feeling as though the mind goes blank
- Irritability (which may or may not be observable to others)
- Increased muscle aches or soreness
- Difficulty sleeping (due to trouble falling asleep or staying asleep, restlessness at night, or unsatisfying sleep)

Many people suffering from GAD also experience the following symptoms:

- Sweating
- Nausea
- Diarrhea

However, diagnosis can be an imperfect science, and other medical conditions, lifestyle choices (including excessive alcohol consumption, cannabis and drug use, and undiagnosed traumas) can also lead to similar symptoms.

YOUR ANXIETY RESCUE

If you are struggling with excessive worry, which makes it hard to carry out day-to-day activities and responsibilities or increasingly leads you to feel depressed, some of the solutions that follow may be just the rescue remedy you need.

But like any medicine, you do have to take action.

For example, part of my self-care plan includes many of the things we'll discuss in *Anxiety Rescue,* including regular:

- Massage
- Talk-therapy or counselling

- Time alone
- Prayer
- Meditation
- Low consumption of alcohol
- Defragging from social media regularly
- Journaling

IN THE NEXT CHAPTER, we'll look at some of the ways anxiety is treated, including the growing discontent with pharmaceutical attempts to 'cure' anxiety versus natural ways to increase serotonin and other feel-good hormones in the body-brain.

2

TREATING ANXIETY

As Edmund J. Bourne (Ph.D.) writes in the preface to the Third Edition of *The Anxiety & Phobia Workbook,* there have been several noteworthy changes in the treatment of anxiety disorders. A major shift has been "to give prescription medication more preference, especially when anxiety symptoms are in the *moderate* to *severe range.*"

Borne attributes this in part with the increased awareness of "the role of heredity and neurobiology in the *causation* of anxiety disorders."

My personal and professional view is that while medication intervention can be extremely helpful for some, it should be used with some degree of caution. Part of that caution involves increasing the awareness of how it may be too readily prescribed without a comprehensive analysis of lifestyle or temporary stressors that may be impacting anxiety levels.

And we'll discuss throughout *Anxiety Rescue, how* in our Western culture, so many people drink excessively, use recreational drugs, overwork, bottle up their feelings, lead sedentary lives, don't switch off, endure toxic and narcissistic relationships, have undiagnosed and untreated trauma—and a vast range of other factors that can lead to excessive worry and anxiety.

Even with the best intentions, a 15-minute doctor's visit will seldom unearth these triggers and certainly won't heal them. Some therapists have suggested it can take up to three months of repeated visits before clients feel comfortable and safe enough to reveal the real sources of their anxiety.

Intimacy takes time. Which explains, in part, why prescription medication has become the drug of choice.

While any approach that relieves suffering should be utilized science has sometimes been at odds with the notion that people can cure themselves.

I'm also increasingly alarmed by the side effects that many of my clients suffer—including depression and suicidal thoughts. Others, just feel tired, lethargic, and demotivated. Some become fat.

In the pages that follow, my intent is to provide ideas, strategies, and suggestions that have been helpful for me personally and for my clients. However, as I'm sure you appreciate they are not intended as a substitute for psychotherapy, counseling, or consulting with your physician.

As a holistic therapist and life coach I know there is a wide range of alternative healing approaches that yield remarkable, extremely quick results. It concerns me, and a lot of other health professionals, that too often people turn to anti-anxiety and antidepressant medication, despite research that cites the lower effectiveness and adverse side-effects.

For many people, this still appears to be the solution of choice prescribed by many medical professions.

"Pills are cheap," my doctor told me when I asked her why counseling and therapy weren't recommended to more people. It may be cheap, but worryingly it is not always effective and the side-effects can also do more harm than healing.

MASKING PAIN DOES NOT OFFER LONG-TERM RELIEF

Rather than offer short-term help very often people come to rely on medical prescriptions for decades. In an extract from his book, *Lost Connections: Uncovering The Real Causes of Depression – and the Unexpected Solutions,* Johann Hari, who took antidepressants for 13 years, says masking the pain does not offer long-term relief and calls for a new approach.

> "I was a teenager when I swallowed my first antidepressant. I was standing in the weak English sunshine, outside a pharmacy in a shopping centre in London. The tablet was white and small, and as I swallowed, it felt like a chemical kiss," Hari says.
>
> "That morning I had gone to see my doctor and I had told him – crouched, embarrassed – that pain was leaking out of me uncontrollably, like a bad smell, and I had felt this way for several years. In reply, he told me a story.
>
> "'There is a chemical called serotonin that makes people feel good, he said, and some people are naturally lacking it in their brains. You are clearly one of those people. There are now, thankfully, new drugs that will restore your serotonin level to that of a normal person. Take them, and you will be well.'
>
> "At last, I understood what had been happening to me, and why. However, a few months into my drugging, something odd happened. The pain started to seep through again. Before long, I felt as bad as I had at the start.
>
> "I went back to my doctor, and he told me that I was clearly on too low a dose. And so, 20 milligrams became 30 milligrams; the white pill became blue. I felt better for several months. And then the pain came back through once more. My dose kept being jacked up, until I was on 80mg, where it stayed for many years, with only a few short breaks. And still the pain broke back through."

You can read a summary of Hari's views, including his claims of an over-riding profit motive by pharmaceutical companies, in his interview with *The Guardian*. <u>'Is everything you think you know about depression wrong?'</u>

A GOOD THERAPIST will often share strategies that can help you rebalance the hormones in your brain, or refer you to other health professionals like nutritionists and dietitians.

As you'll discover in *Anxiety Rescue*, there are numerous ways to increase serotonin in your brain without drugs— meditation, exercise, sunlight, vitamins and other low-cost approaches.

Many of these strategies will save you money, boost your health, help you reduce weight and improve your relationships. Eliminating or cutting back alcohol consumption is one effective lifestyle habit I discuss in the chapter 'Mindful Drinking'.

<u>Alcohol has been found to significantly reduce serotonin 45 minutes after drinking</u>. As this article in *SpiritScience* claims, there is also a clear link between alcohol consumption, anger, violence, suicide and other types of aggressive behavior. Aggression is also heavily linked to low serotonin levels and may be due to alcohol's disrupting effects on serotonin metabolism.

In New Zealand, where talk-therapy or counseling was once generously funded by the Government, several years ago this was diverted to the seemingly more (cost) effective method of prescription medicine. Interestingly, in 2019, moves are afoot to rewrite the imbalance and provide more mental health services, including counseling.

As Bourne also notes, "As a counterpoint to prescription medications, there has also been an increased interest in the use of herbs and natural agents to reduce anxiety. I believe these substances can be quite helpful —some more for anxiety, some more for depression—when such problems are in the *mild* to *moderate* range of severity."

HOLISTIC HEALTH

I first met Alice Morris in 1997 when I went in search of something to help alleviate my soaring stress levels. Other recruitment consultants I worked with at the Global Recruitment agency, where I later developed shingles, swore by her holistic healing approach.

Back in the 90s, her approach was innovative—considered almost heretical in the eyes of the mainstream medical profession. Now, much of what she offers, including acupuncture, has been scientifically validated and embraced.

Alice and her multifaceted approach to managing acute anxiety and toxic stress was my first introduction to mind, body, and soul healing.

And it helped. It helped a lot. Especially her massage, acupuncture, and some of the herbs she prescribed for me.

However, as you'll learn in *Anxiety Rescue* unless the root cause is addressed, i.e. my toxic work situation, Alice's approach, as with any other, just helped me tread water for a little longer.

When my nervous system finally yelled, "Pay Attention," and I developed shingles, I knew I could no longer lie to myself. I knew I had to leave my job. I share my exact strategy and more of my story in my *Mid-Life Career Rescue* series of books.

As you'll read from Alice's story, she also left a less than ideal, yet esteemed career, to follow her true calling. I am grateful to Alice—I credit her work with helping me regain control of the reins of my anxiety and to helping me stay alive. Her approach to health and well-being restored me to strength until such time as I could leave my job.

> "My parents wanted me to be secure in my life in China and their expectations like most Chinese parents were for their children to get a good education and get a high position job so I studied accountancy for 5 years and worked for a big wholesale electrical appliance company as a senior accountant, a job position in which I was the envy of many people at the time.

Even though this was a very successful job and I was considered a success I was not happy in doing it.

In 1990 at the age of 29, I decided to move to New Zealand to follow my dream of understanding true health. This was the perfect opportunity to start doing Chinese medicine again. I worked in Auckland for 4 years doing herbs and acupressure.

In 1995 I set up the Wellington Health Massage Clinic followed by the Alice Qigong and Acupressure school. I also returned to China frequently from 1996 studying in Xanxi ,Fujian, Anhui, Tai Yuan in Qigong, Fung shui, Chinese Astrology and medicine.

In 2007 I completed an advanced two-month course in Beijing on food healing formulas with Professor Liu who has over 270 branches in China and is one of the leading authorities of the ancient Chinese food healing techniques which is having outstanding results in mainland China.

Through this work I found the New Zealand climate and culture was quite different from China so I had to adjust my treatment according to New Zealand conditions and realised that including Herbs, acupressure, and acupuncture is not enough.

I have found peoples health is not just what the traditional healing methods of acupuncture, acupressure and herbs is but far more including their beliefs, what food they eat, their working state, family state, living environment, general health constitution, lifestyle and their time and date of birth (Chinese Astrology).

A holistic approach is a much deeper way of addressing your health."

Throughout *Anxiety Rescue* you'll discover a range of natural antidepressants and anxiety-reducing strategies. Importantly, you'll learn empowering strategies that will help you be less dependent on the drug companies and more in control of you and your life.

My hope is that in the process you will experience a feeling of profound joy and peace—a 'feeling of being at home' and reclaiming what you once felt was lost, broken, or missing from your life.

But first, let's try and pinpoint just what's making you anxious.

3

WHAT MAKES YOU ANXIOUS?

Sometimes when you name the beast you can tame the beast.

Here are just a few of many things that can increase feelings of anxiety:

- Mounting debt
- Job loss
- Burnout and stress
- Relationship issues
- Conflict at work
- Public speaking
- Exams and performance appraisals
- Bullying
- Toxic people
- Narcissism
- Trauma
- Fear

Here are a few other common culprits:

- Career dissatisfaction (the job itself, overwork)
- Colleagues or bosses at work

- Health (depression, self-image, weight, illness, etc.)
- Environmental (noise, weather, chaos, etc.)
- Toxic work environments
- Financial uncertainty
- Values conflicts
- Uncertainty
- Change (keeping up with technology)
- Information obesity/overload
- Bombardment/decision fatigue
- Cumulative stress
- The political climate/leadership fears

Lifestyle and health choices can also increase feelings of anxiety:

- Alcohol consumption and drug use
- Poor diet
- Vitamin deficiencies
- Lack of exercise
- Technology use, including phone overuse
- Social media
- Lack of, or disrupted, sleep
- Lack of work-life balance

Chemical imbalances in your brain and gut may also be the culprit. Including too much or too little:

- Serotonin
- Dopamine
- Norepinephrine
- Noradrenaline
- And other chemicals, hormones and neurotransmitters

If you're wondering if the symptoms you're having are caused by a chemical imbalance, it's important to know that there's quite a bit of controversy surrounding this theory.

In fact, it's been largely refuted by the medical community. Researchers argue that the chemical imbalance hypothesis is more of a figure of speech.

It doesn't really capture the true complexity of these disorders. In other words, anxiety and other mental disorders aren't simply caused by chemical imbalances in the brain. As I've already highlighted, there's a lot more complexity to them, and there's also a myriad of natural ways to correct any imbalance.

The chemical imbalance theory also doesn't explain how these chemicals become unbalanced in the first place.

As Harvard Medical School reports, there are likely millions of different chemical reactions occurring in your brain at any given time. These are responsible for your mood and overall feelings. It's impossible to tell if anyone truly has a chemical imbalance in their brain at a given time.

The most common evidence used to support the chemical imbalance theory is the effectiveness of anti-anxiety and anti-depressant medications. These medications work by increasing the amounts of serotonin and other neurotransmitters in the brain.

However, just because your mood can be elevated with drugs that increase brain chemicals doesn't mean that your symptoms were caused by a deficiency in that chemical in the first place. It's just as possible that low serotonin levels are just another symptom of depression, not the cause.

There are no reliable tests to identify imbalances in your brain. Firstly, not all neurotransmitters are produced in the brain. Secondly, neurotransmitter levels in your body and brain are constantly and rapidly changing. This makes tests unreliable.

Thyroid and other disorders can also trigger symptoms of anxiety and other mental disorders.

When it comes to anxiety, there are likely many factors at play. As, you'll discover in the next chapter, even some of the most successful people can suffer from, and recover from, crippling anxiety.

4

ANXIETY FOR ALL

Every human being feels anxious at sometime. According to the National Survey of Mental Health and Wellbeing conducted by the Australian Bureau of Statistics anxiety is the most common mental condition in Australia.

Remember, different people are anxious in different ways. Many people think that being anxious only means being nervous, fearful, or tearful.

This isn't true at all. Many anxious people are quiet, withdrawn or reserved. Other anxious people become angry and enraged.

Some people feel they are going insane.

Anxious people come in all shapes, sizes, and ages. You can become anxious at any age and stage of your life.

Some of the most wildly successful and outwardly confident people suffer from anxiety. Lady Gaga, Robbie Williams, Duff McKagan—and other great performers are just some of the many superstars who suffer from this mental illness.

It might, I suggest, surprise people to hear that the charismatic and mega-talented actress and musician Lady Gaga feels anxious about anything. Recently, as I was, she was given a diagnosis of Post Traumatic Stress Disorder. I suspect the more accurate diagnosis would be Complex Trauma, given the many traumatic situations she has experienced.

Gaga says that taming her anxiety and regulating her nervous system takes daily effort.

> "So that I don't panic over circumstances that to many would seem like normal life situations. Examples are leaving the house or being touched by strangers who simply want to share their enthusiasm for my music.
>
> I also struggle with triggers from the memories I carry from my feelings of past years on tour when my needs and requests for balance were being ignored.
>
> I was overworked and not taken seriously when I shared my pain and concern that something was wrong. I ultimately ended up injured on the *Born This Way Ball*.
>
> That moment and the memory of it has changed my life forever. The experience of performing night after night in mental and physical pain ingrained in me a trauma that I relive when I see or hear things that remind me of those days.
>
> I also experience something called dissociation which means that my mind doesn't want to relive the pain so 'I look off and I stare' in a glazed over state… My body is in one place and my mind in another. It's like the panic accelerator in my mind gets stuck and I am paralyzed with fear.
>
> When this happens I can't talk. When this happens repeatedly, it makes me have a common PTSD reaction which is that I feel depressed and unable to function like I used to. It's harder to do my job. It's harder to do simple things like take a shower. Everything has become harder.
>
> Additionally, when I am unable to regulate my anxiety, it can result

in somatization, which is pain in the body caused by an inability to express my emotional pain in words."

She engages with various modalities of psychotherapy to manage symptoms of dissociation and PTSD, that threatened to derail her life before she found her vibe tribe which included mental health support.

When the trauma of her high school bullying and sexual assault was left untreated she said it, "later morphed into physical chronic pain, fibromyalgia, panic attacks, acute trauma responses, and debilitating mental spirals that have included the suicidal ideation and masochistic behavior. Okay. I'm done with my list, but that list changed my life. And it changed my life not in a good way."

"I'm telling you this because for me it was too late," she said. "I needed help earlier. I needed mental health care. I needed someone to see not through me or see the star that I'd become but rather see the darkness inside that I was struggling with."

With her health now manageable, she wants to use her experience to make sure it doesn't happen to anyone else.

> "I wish I had mental health resources then because although what I have is treatable and can hopefully and will get better over time, if there was preventative mental healthcare accessible to me earlier, I believe it might not have gotten as bad as it did," she said. "I wish there had been a system in place to protect and guide me. A system in place to empower me to say no to things I felt I had to do. A system in place to empower me to stay away from toxic working environments or working with people that were of seriously questionable character."

You'll find a plethora of health resources throughout the *Anxiety Rescue* series.

5

HOW DOES ANXIETY IMPACT YOU?

Common signs of anxiety can include, fear, headaches, insomnia, tiredness, depression, anger, and irritability.

The body never lies. However, many people soldier on ignoring the obvious warning signs their body is giving them.

When you feel anxious your body overflows with oxygen and adrenaline. Your heart can race. Your body can mimic a heart attack.

It's easy to worry about these feelings and think you're going to die. But the reality is your body is just trying to protect you from what it thinks is danger, even though you don't need protecting. This is because of the toxic levels of stress in your body.

PHYSICAL SIGNS OF ANXIETY

- Increased heart rate
- Pounding heart
- Sweaty palms
- Elevated blood pressure
- Tightness of the chest, neck, jaw and back muscles

- Headache
- Diarrhea
- Constipation
- Unable to pass urine or incontinence
- Trembling
- Twitching
- Stuttering and other speech difficulties
- Nausea
- Vomiting
- Sleep disturbances
- Fatigue
- Being easily startled
- Shallow, rapid breathing
- Dryness of mouth or throat
- Cold hands
- Susceptibility to minor illnesses
- Itching
- Chronic pain
- Sore eyes

EMOTIONAL SIGNS OF ANXIETY

- Fear
- Tearful
- Impatience
- Frightened
- Moody
- Highs and lows
- Feeling of loss/grief
- Depression
- Anger
- Irritability
- Short-tempered
- Sadness
- Rage

- Being Hyper-Critical

COGNITIVE SIGNS OF ANXIETY

- Racing thoughts
- Forgetfulness
- Preoccupation
- Errors in judging distance/space
- Diminished or exaggerated fantasy life
- Reduced creativity
- Lack of concentration
- Diminished productivity
- Lack of attention to detail
- Orientation to the past
- Diminished reaction time
- Clumsiness
- Disorganization of thoughts
- Negative self-esteem
- Negative self-statements
- Diminished sense of meaning in life
- Lack of control/need for too much control
- Negative evaluation of experiences

BEHAVIORAL SIGNS OF ANXIETY

- Avoidance
- Carelessness
- Under-eating – leading to excessive weight loss
- Over-eating – leading to weight gain
- Aggressiveness
- Increased smoking/starting smoking
- Withdrawal
- Argumentative
- Increased alcohol or drug use

- Listlessness
- Hostility
- Accident prone
- Nervous laughter
- Compulsive behavior
- Impatience
- Agitation

Social signs of anxiety

- Relationship difficulties
- Increased conflicts
- Marital issues
- Alienation/withdrawal
- Domestic violence
- Alcohol and substance abuse

Spiritual signs of stress

- Hopelessness
- Doubting of values and beliefs
- Withdrawing from fellowship or group support
- Decreased spiritual practices (i.e. prayer, meditation, yoga etc)
- Becoming angry or bitter at a higher power or God
- Loss of compassion —for self and others

It's important to make yourself the boss of your body again. Keep an eye out for any warning signs your body barometer may give you in the future.

When you feel calm what do you notice? How does this differ from times when you are anxious? Sometimes you can 'fake it to make it'—by tricking your body to relax, thinking calming thoughts, stimulating energizing emotions, and engaging in spiritually healing techniques you can restore your mind, body, and spirit to calm.

As always, proactive, not reactive, care is the best strategy. Don't wait too long. And keep up the daily wellbeing practices you'll discover throughout this book.

6

YOUR BRILLIANT BODY—NATURAL MOOD-ENHANCING DRUGS

Did you know you have your own drug company? One capable of delivering tremendous relief, and infinitely able to naturally heal anxiety, depression, and a range of other mental imbalances.

Yes, your brilliant body can heal—with a little help.

SEROTONIN AND DOPAMINE Deficiency

Life is bleak when you are low on serotonin, dopamine and other feel-good neurotransmitters. Anxiety, depression, pessimism, and aggression can all come calling.

Thankfully there are natural ways to increase your mood, including:

- Meditation
- Positive thoughts
- Exercise
- Social Dominance
- Sunlight
- Light therapy
- Amino Acids

- Low GI Carbs
- Omega 3
- Gut Bacteria
- Spices—including turmeric
- Limiting or eliminating alcohol

Throughout *Anxiety Rescue*, I'll share a smorgasbord of strategies to reduce anxiety naturally.

I'm not offering a miracle cure, and by no means do I provide an exhaustive list. But I am sharing what's worked for me and the thousands of clients I have helped professionally in my role as a therapist and holistic counselor.

Best of all many of these strategies are inexpensive and all readily within reach. Many, if not all, are infinitely enjoyable. You'll gain a natural high that keeps on giving.

I

BOOK ONE: LEONARDO DA VINCI

AUTHOR'S NOTE

Realize that everything connects to everything else.

~ Leonardo da Vinci

Leonardo was just like you and I. He suffered at times from self-doubt, he had family hassles, some of his efforts resulted in failure, people jealous of his talent tried to undermine him, money worries meant that at times he had to suck it up and do work he didn't enjoy, and he had to work for bullies and tyrants.

But he didn't let obstacles stop him from doing the work he loved. The pursuit of knowledge born of his own enquiry and experience ultimately led to his success. He also learned from experts he admired, both past and present.

The success secrets and strategies of extraordinary artists like Leonardo da Vinci can help people like you and I succeed—personally and professionally. Successful artists have always struggled, but they persevered anyway. And it is this willingness to pursue their calling in the face of many challenges that holds lessons for us all.

HOW THIS BOOK WILL HELP YOU

Whenever I'm in a slump or needing an inspirational boost I turn to people who are smarter or more skilled than me for good advice.

I've done the same with qualities I've wanted to develop, like patience. "What would Mother Theresa do now?" I asked many years ago. Mother Theresa wouldn't shout! She wouldn't lose her cool. She'd send loving kindness and smile. And that's what I did whenever I got frustrated.

If you've been procrastinating, experiencing self-doubt, feeling fearful, or just getting in your own way, you're in good company, Leonardo's been there. I've been there too—as have many successful people. Guess what, getting in your own way is normal!

I promise there are solutions to the problems you're currently facing—and you'll find them in the pages that follow.

Dig into this book and let Leonardo da Vinci be your mentor, inspiration and guide as he calls forth your passions, purpose and potential.

Through the teachings of Leonardo, extensive research into the mysteries of motivation, success and fulfillment, and my own personal experience and professional success with clients as a holistic therapist, *Anxiety Rescue* will help you accelerate success. Together, Leonardo and I will guide you to where you need to go next, and give you practical steps to tame anxiety, beat worry, minimize stress and achieve success.

PRINCIPLE ONE: THE CALL FOR SUCCESS

WHAT IS SUCCESS?

I wish to work miracles.

-Leonardo da Vinci

Modern definitions of success are often too narrowly defined. Success is more than climbing up the corporate ladder. It's more than a big shiny car, or owning the latest and greatest. It's more than the number of likes you have on Facebook.

Success includes maintaining good health, energy and enthusiasm for life, fulfilling relationships, creative freedom, well-being, peace of mind, happiness and joy. Success also includes the ability to achieve your desires—whatever these may be.

Success is living life on your terms.

Leonardo was driven to self-actualize—to fulfill his talents and potential, and achieve his life purpose.

Success meant following his curiosity and the freedom to think, be and do as he chose. His success came from creatively expressing his most important beliefs and values, and sharing his knowledge with the world.

YOUR CHALLENGE

What does success mean to you?

How will you know when you have succeeded?

> *Imagine how our culture, how our lives, will change when we begin valuing go-givers as much as we value go-getters.*
>
> ~ Arianna Huffington, businesswoman

WHAT CAN SUCCESS DO?

The caterpillar which through the care exercised in weaving round itself its new habitation with admirable design and ingenious workmanship, afterwards emerges from it with beautiful painted wings, rising on these towards heaven.

~ Leonardo da Vinci

Many people struggle to achieve because they're not motivated by success. But being successful isn't just about obtaining worldly possessions, status or glory.

Success is achieved by putting energy and effort toward something you desire. Knowing why you want something is just as important as knowing what you want.

ACHIEVING SUCCESS ON YOUR TERMS:

- Helps you lead a richer life
- Is an indispensable part of fulfillment
- Helps you grow
- Energizes you
- Liberates you
- Opens up fresh horizons
- Boosts your health and helps you live longer
- Will change your life and the lives of those who matter most to you

YOUR CHALLENGE

Why is succeeding important to you?

My mother would always remind me: 'Where you are is not who you are.' I grew up in a poor neighborhood in New York City. My mother saw education as the way up and out for her children. It didn't take long for me to see the wisdom in her beliefs.

~ Ursula Burns, engineer and CEO

SUCCESS FOR ALL

Remember to acquire diligence rather than rapidity.

~ Leonardo da Vinci

Everybody is capable of success, but many people think they're not. Some people believe they're too young to be taken seriously; others that when they hit midlife they've left it too late to succeed.

Successful people come in all shapes, races, ages and stages. And sometimes the greatest successes follow the greatest failures.

To succeed you have to believe it's possible for you—even if it means faking it until you make it and realize it's true. A slow and bumpy road is the route to success for many.

Leonardo's seemingly meteoric rise to success was based on slow, incremental steps, dodging obstacles, fueled by self-belief and constant and earnest effort.

YOUR CHALLENGE

What great works might reside inside of you?

What steps, no matter how small, could you begin to take?

Your success will not be determined by your gender or your ethnicity, but only on the scope of your dreams and your hard work to achieve them.

~ Dame Zaha Mohammad Hadid, architect

YOU'RE NEVER TOO OLD OR YOUNG TO MAKE IT BIG

What is fair in men, passes away, but not so in art.

~ Leonardo da Vinci

You're never too old to become legendary. At the time of writing this book Leonardo is forever young at 564—immortalized in our minds and hearts and still impacting science, technology and creativity.

He never let age define his potential for success. He was fifteen when he was apprenticed to Andrea del Verrocchio in 1467—considered old at the time to start his career.

Leonardo was 37 when he began studying anatomy in 1489; 43 when he began The Last Supper in 1495; 44 when he illustrated mathematician Fra Luca Pacioli's *De divina proportione* (On the Divine Proportion).

He was 46 when he attempted a flying machine; 50 when he became Cesare Borgia's military engineer; and 51 when he began the Mona Lisa in 1503.

At the 'old' age of 55 Leonardo was appointed court painter and engineer by Louis XII, King of France. When he began his last known work and one of his most enigmatic and famous paintings, St John the Baptist, he was 63. Only a few years later, aged 67 he would die legend says, peacefully in the arms of the King of France. And he's still making it big!

YOUR CHALLENGE

If you believe your age is a barrier to success look for examples where the opposite is true

I never thought I'd be successful. It seems in my own mind that in everything I've undertaken I've never quite made the mark. But I've always been able to put disappointments aside. Success isn't about the end result; it's about what you learn along the way.

~ Vera Wang, fashion designer

REALITY CHECK ON SUCCESS

*No sooner is Virtue born than Envy
comes into the world to attack it.*

~ Leonardo da Vinci

Success is not always fun. Like anything worthwhile, pursuing success often involves great commitment, hard work and sacrifice.

Successful people are prepared to give up things, albeit it temporarily, to live a more passionate and prosperous life. Successful people are prepared to stand out from the crowd, take risks and cope with failure.

The journey to success isn't always glamorous; it's often hard work, with long hours, little thanks and creeping doubt that anyone will appreciate the tireless effort you so passionately put into what you do. You may be, as Leonardo was, attacked by those envious of your achievements.

But the compensation is a bigger, fuller, more interesting life, and the potential to create an enduring legacy.

YOUR CHALLENGE

What are you prepared to trade-off to be more successful?

What are you prepared to change in your life? What would stop you?

Reserve your right to think, for even to think wrongly is better than not to think at all.

~ Hypatia of Alexandria, astronomer

YOUR BODY BAROMETER

The deeper the feeling, the greater the pain.

~ Leonardo da Vinci

The more you truly care about something, the deeper the consequences can be when you don't act on your desires.

When you aren't true to yourself and you don't do the things you aspire to do your mental, emotional and spiritual health can suffer.

Common signs of neglecting the call for success and forsaking your ambitions can include: tiredness, depression, anxiety, irritability, and strained personal relationships. In short, you're lovesick—starved of the things that spark joy.

The body never lies, but many people soldier on ignoring the obvious warning signs. It's easy to rationalize these feelings away, But the reality is your mind, body and soul is screaming out for more. Have the courage to say 'yes' to pursuing a more liberating alternative.

YOUR CHALLENGE

When you feel unfulfilled, bored, unchallenged and demotivated what do you notice? How does this differ from times when you feel the fear but love life passionately anyway?

I've been absolutely terrified every moment of my life—and I've never let it keep me from doing a single thing I wanted to do.

~ Georgia O'Keeffe, artist

LIVE A SIGNIFICANT LIFE

No counsel is more trustworthy than that which is given upon ships that are in peril.

~ Leonardo da Vinci

Regret because of a life not lived significantly is a major source of depression, stress and anger for many people.

You only get one shot at life. Don't spend it regretting opportunities you never took and dreams you never lived. Turn moments of peril into catalysts for change in your quest for significance.

Leonardo was often in peril but he mastered the art of creating solutions and turning calamity into good fortune.

That's not to say there weren't days when he truly despaired, when his attempts at innovation failed, when invaders overran the cities where he lived forcing him to flee, when his creations were rejected, destroyed or had to be abandoned.

During all these times, fueled by his desire to live a significant life, he kept moving forward.

YOUR CHALLENGE

How could exposure to injury, loss or destruction fuel your motivation to succeed?

If you only had one year to live what would you regret never having been or done? How can you heed the call for significance and pursue your heart's desire?

I believe that every single event in life happens in an opportunity to choose love over fear.

~ Oprah, businesswoman

ESCAPE THE COMFORT RUT

You will never have a greater or lesser dominion than that over yourself...the height of a man's success is gauged by his self-mastery.

~ Leonardo da Vinci

Many people trade off their deeper passions for material comforts and status that can only ever give fleeting satisfaction. Others get stuck in the comfort rut, trapped by the familiarity of what they know. Outwardly, they appear successful but in fact they are deeply unfulfilled.

We all like to be comfortable, but the comfort rut is like wearing old shoes—you just keep putting them on because they feel familiar. But in the deepest part of your heart you know they're full of holes.

Are you too comfortable—stagnating, not growing, nor challenging or exciting yourself? Perhaps it's the fear of the unknown, or starting over, failing or succeeding. Fear is part of the human condition. It reminds you you're alive. But it doesn't have to stop you from succeeding.

Leonardo continually reinvented himself. He strove to master himself

—his thoughts, his emotions, his behaviors throughout the change process.

Success equalled growth, aligning with his soul's purpose, taking inspired action he found interesting, meaningful, fulfilling and intriguing.

Being true to your self, and honoring the passion of your soul, can be the most comfortable feeling of all.

YOUR CHALLENGE

How will fulfilling your potential feel to you? How could gaining more self-mastery benefit your life and boost your success?

I will never give myself the luxury of thinking 'I've made it.' I'm not the same as I was 20 years ago, but I always set the bar higher.

~ Dame Zaha Mohammad Hadid, architect

PRINCIPLE TWO: EMPOWER YOUR SUCCESS

THE POWER OF PASSION

If there's no love, what then?

~ Leonardo da Vinci

Without love you don't have energy. Without energy you have nothing.

When people are pursuing something they are passionate about their drive and determination is infinite. They become like pieces of elastic able to stretch to anything and accommodate any setback. People immobilized by fear and passivity snap like a twig. They lack resilience.

Passion gives people a reason for living and the confidence and drive to pursue their dreams. Leonardo was a man of many loves and deep obsessions. These passions imbued him with infinite energy—powering his creativity, courage, resolve and tenacity.

As Leonardo once said, "No labour is sufficient to tire me."

Even when he was exhausted by life, his passion sustained him.

YOUR CHALLENGE

What will passion do for you?

The really important stuff is not in my résumé. It's what has gone on almost unnoticed in the secret chambers of the heart.

~ Isabel Allende, author

FIND YOUR ELEMENT

Why go about puffed up and pompous, dressed and decorated with [the fruits], not of their own labors, but of those of others.

~ Leonardo da Vinci

Leonardo's father recognized his exceptional gift for drawing and helped him hone his talent by apprenticing him to Andrea del Verrocchio, a master painter, sculptor and engineer.

However Leonardo also self-taught his way to excellence, learning new skills and tackling subjects he passionately wanted to understand but had little knowledge of.

Have you found your point of brilliance? Maybe you're exceptional in drawing, dancing, cooking, or some other field. If that talent is combined with your deepest interests, values, ambitions and joy that's where you ought to focus.

Whether you know your elemental strengths already or you're at a loss, it's equally important to try new things.

If you don't branch out from what you have already mastered you cannot grow. You may discover a point of brilliance you never knew you possessed. In humans, as there is in hills, sometimes there's a vein of gold that you never knew you owned.

YOUR CHALLENGE

One way to discover your strongest skills and natural talents is to ask people close to you, "What's my superpower?"

Notice all the things you love to do while expressing your unique talents and list past activities and accomplishments that accurately reflect these abilities

What are some possible ways that expressing your qualities, talents and skills may fulfill current or future needs. How can you serve?

Pick the places that you want to be great, that you want to focus your energies on and do that—understanding that you're probably not going to be great at everything.

~ Ursula Burns, CEO

YOUR SOUL'S DESIRE

Men who desire nothing but material riches are absolutely devoid of that wisdom which is the food and the only true riches of the mind. So much worthier is the soul than the body, so much nobler are the possessions of the soul than those of the body.

~ Leonardo da Vinci

Leonardo described himself as an inventor—it was fundamental to his success. He was a visionary, always searching to understand what was and what could be. In his quest to create and invent he sought knowledge and wisdom above all else. He sought to fill his soul and he sought to be of service to the world, advancing science and other realms in the process.

Acquiring material riches wasn't high on his list of priorities. In life as in chess forethought wins. Decide what you really want, what you are prepared to give up for it and what your priorities will be.

YOUR CHALLENGE

If you're struggling to clarify what it is you really want notice the times your soul comes alive. Notice what excites and interests you, and keep these clues to passion in an inspirational journal.

Passion, love, bliss or joy—whatever name it goes by—is hard to define but easy to see and feel. Your body will change quickly when the richness of your soul finds you.

Here's just a few of her clues:

- A burning desire, hunger, sense of excitement or feeling of inspiration
- A state of arousal—a racing heart, light-headedness, sweaty palms, butterflies, breathlessness
- A feeling of limitless energy
- A clarity of vision
- A sense of purpose and caring deeply
- A feeling of contentment.

*I don't believe you can ever really cook
unless you love eating.*

~ Nigella Lawson, celebrity chef

ACQUIRE KNOWLEDGE

Learning never exhausts the mind.

~ Leonardo da Vinci

Leonardo was driven to understand how things worked. Through his understanding he was able to excel in his chosen fields, innovate and achieve what many believed impossible.

By studying how birds flew he prophesied one day, 'Man will fly through the air but will not move.' Isn't that what we do when we sit on a plane?

He devoured so many sources of knowledge including: reading ancient texts, studying people and places, writing and drawing to deepen his understanding, hands-on knowledge: making models, prototypes, post-mortem examination, experimentation, traveling and learning about others cultures, mentors—past and present, studying artifacts and symbols, and channelling divine intelligence.

YOUR CHALLENGE

To achieve success take a leaf out of Leonardo's journal and acquire knowledge; self-knowledge; knowledge of others you admire; knowledge of the people, places, things that fascinate, excite, intrigue, or arouse your curiosity

Gain new knowledge by breaking free of your comfort rut and seek new experiences. Be experimental. It may take a few different experiences to finally find your happy place.

One of the greatest gifts my brother and I received from my mother was her love of literature and language. With their boundless energy, libraries open the door to these worlds and so many others.

~ Caroline Herschel, astronomer

TEACH WHAT YOU WANT TO LEARN

*Feathers will raise men,
as they do birds toward heaven.*

~ Leonardo da Vinci

Leonardo found purpose and fulfillment in teaching. As have other extremely successful men and women in possession of curious minds, and ennobled with a love of learning. Polymath Tim Ferris, for example, sees himself not as a wealthy entrepreneur but as a teacher.

"It's not how much money we make that ultimately makes us happy between nine and five. It's whether or not our work fulfills us. Being a teacher is meaningful," Malcolm Gladwell writes in *Outliers: The Story of Success.*

Leonardo's feathers of higher learning were the quills with which he wrote his notes. He believed, and knew from experience, the tremendous power of books and words to create miraculous flights of the mind.

He wrote about what he wanted to learn, and found extraordinary success, sharing that knowledge with others.

In coaching and counseling sessions with clients when they say they don't know how to get unstuck, or how to find answers, I gently encourage them to consider writing a blog post I, or they, could share with other people who may also be stuck. It's incredible how the thought of helping others motivates them. And in turn, they help themselves.

YOUR CHALLENGE

Teach what you want to learn—blog, video, paint, write a song or piece of music, write a book or create some art, create a course, host a seminar or speak at a conference or forum, Youtube or anything else that inspires and challenges you

Enjoy the 'helper's high'—the flow of positive endorphins when you step out of your comfort zone and inspire others

> *Let us remember: One book, one pen, one child, and one teacher can change the world.*
>
> ~ Malala Yousafzai, Noble Peace laureate

LOVE FERVENTLY

The love of anything is the offspring of knowledge, love being more fervent in proportion as knowledge is more certain.

~ Leonardo da Vinci

Conventional science teaches that the main role of the heart is to pump blood around your body. But that's just a tiny part of the heart's power.

Your heart has an intelligence far greater than the brain. Scientific studies also confirm that your heart has the biggest and most powerful electromagnetic field.

But the heart, like any major organ needs nourishment to perform miracles. Feed and oxygenate your heart with all the things you love.

True fervent love is not something you can turn on and off like a tap. It is an obsession so consuming it feeds your soul. It can be as tangible as a vocation, or a house or as intangible as a dream or an idea. You could be in love with anything.

Here's a few of the things Leonardo loved with a passion:

- Knowledge
- A cause
- Analyzing and understanding things
- Books
- Technology
- The future
- A belief
- An idea
- Freedom

YOUR CHALLENGE

What captures your heart's interest and attention? List as many things as you can that you love passionately

People feed off passions—not professions. Become a Love Mark and magnetize opportunities toward you. You may want to read more about how to be a love mark in my book Mid-Life Career Rescue: Employ Yourself—getBook.at/EmployYourself

> *I think sometimes that people assume because I'm on television I'm an expert, but I think the whole point of what I do is that I'm not and I don't have any training. My approach isn't about a fancy ingredient or style. I cook what I love to eat.*
>
> ~ Nigella Lawson, celebrity chef

UNDERSTAND THE RULES

He who loves practice without theory is like the sailor who boards a ship without a rudder and compass and never knows where he may cast.

~ Leonardo da Vinci

If you want to fast-track your success in any endeavor you need to understand the tried-and-proven rules of your chosen field or object of affection.

Leonardo excelled by zealously studying, testing and documenting everything he wanted to master. Always questioning everything, he would take knowledge commonly held to be true and subject it to his own rigorous experimentation.

At times he would disregard the rules entirely, innovating and breaking new ground, and sometimes failing before discovering success.

In this way he pioneered new discoveries, continually improved his work, created a point of difference and mastered his domain through his theory-based beliefs, and willingness to systematically experiment.

"I know that many will call this useless work; and they will be those of whom Demetrius declared that he took no more account of the wind that came out their mouth in words, then of that they expelled from their lower parts," Leonardo once challenged.

YOUR CHALLENGE

What rules and principles do you need to learn?

What rules and principles do you need to break?

What evidence-based explanations do you have for the beliefs or rules you follow? How might the opposite also be true? How can you adjust your thinking?

Always believe in your work—it will carry you through any difficult situation, but learn to adjust your thinking every once in a while to fit the moment. Never give up. You won't always get everything right every time —but you have to keep trying. Have the commitment to persevere.

~ Dame Zaha Mohammad Hadid, architect

FIND YOUR PURPOSE

Make your work to be in keeping with your purpose.

~ Leonardo da Vinci

Leonardo found deep meaning and purpose in understanding the natural world, sharing the knowledge he found to be true, and being of service to the advancement of humanity.

In learning more about the human body he aided medical advancements. In learning more about the laws of vision and perspective he was able to bring paintings to life.

By mastering the art of mechanics he sought to protect and aid the defense of cities and people important to him.

Everything he committed to was done with purpose.

Given that you spend so much of your life working and you're living longer too, it's even more important to pursue your calling. Need convincing?

Benefits of working and living with purpose include:

- Tapping into your life's purpose gives you an edge, firing the flames of passion, enthusiasm, drive and initiative needed to succeed
- A sense of purpose can give you the courage, tenacity and clarity of vision needed to thrive
- Purpose fuels the embers of flagging motivation and helps fuel latent dreams
- A sense of purpose can lead you to the work you were born to do
- Discovering your true calling opens you up to the dreams the Universe has for you—bigger than you can dream for yourself.

YOUR CHALLENGE

What life experiences give your life meaning and purpose?

How could your purpose benefit you and others?

It is in giving that I connect with others, with the world and with the divine.

~ Isabel Allende, author

FIND (AND FACE) YOUR WEAKNESS

Look carefully what part is most ill-favored in your person and take particular pains to correct it in your studies.

~ Leonardo da Vinci

Your biggest weakness can be your greatest strength at times, but equally your greatest strength can be your greatest weakness.

The most important step is self-awareness. Knowing exactly where you need to develop skill or minimize ill-effect will help you develop an effective strategy for success.

Arguably, one of Leonardo's flaws was not finishing the things he started. While there may be many valid reasons for this, some say that Leonardo regretted leaving so many things undone.

Georgio Vasari claims shortly before Leonardo died he said, "I have offended God and mankind by not working on my art as I should have done."

Discovering and taming your own weaknesses can be challenging for several reasons. You may lack objectivity. Other people around you may not be willing to give you honest feedback, or you may stubbornly refuse to deal with your flaws.

YOUR CHALLENGE

Conduct your own investigation to decide if your weaknesses are holding you back

Notice what you are avoiding. Sometimes the things you're putting off could be a sign of something you haven't mastered

Analyze feedback. Review and look for patterns in any assessments and feedback from others. Is there a common theme?

Ask for honesty. Explain that you're wanting to work on your areas for development

Study past failures. Look back at things that didn't go so well and work out why you didn't succeed

Handle it. You can't improve unless you're open to critical, constructive feedback. If something in you is triggered, or your self-esteem and confidence is dealt a blow, put energy into learning how to deal positively with criticism

Leonardo wasn't perfect. I'm not perfect. You're not perfect. No one is perfect. There is always room for improvement if you want to grow.

Anyone who achieves a certain level of success is first and foremost competing against themselves. And for me the idea that I could always do better, learn more, learn faster, is something that came from skating. But I carried that with me for the rest of my life.

~ Vera Wang, fashion designer

AFFIRM FOR SUCCESS

Experience is the mother of all Knowledge.

~ Leonardo da Vinci

Leonardo was just like you and I. He made mistakes, faced many obstacles, endured hardships—including envy, false accusations, exile, and the rejection and destruction of many of his most beloved works. And he was human—he experienced self-doubt like the rest of us.

There were times when he may have felt like giving up—and sometimes did. But his courage and persistence to remain true to himself in the face of adversity can inspire us all.

One of the secrets to his success, one that strengthened his will was his use of empowering affirmations. In his notebook he urged himself on:

- I do not depart from my furrow
- Every obstacle is destroyed through rigor
- Obstacles do not bend me
- As you cannot do what you want, want what you can do
- I shall continue

- I am never weary of serving.

Resilience in the face of adversity is a critical determinant of success in business and life.

YOUR CHALLENGE

What affirmations can you create to sustain you in the face of self-doubt or questioning of the value of your efforts? How can you cheer-lead your way to success?

Plant your affirmations deeper by framing them emotionally. Instead of, "Obstacles do not bend me", experiment with "I feel strong in the face of obstacles—they do not bend me." This engages your heart-centre so that deeper, more resilient changes can take root

It was such a depressing time. I didn't look very depressed maybe but it was really dire. I made a conscious decision not to stop, but it could have gone the other way.

~ Dame Zaha Mohammad Hadid, architect

BE AMBITIOUS

Escape the cauldron.

~ Leonardo da Vinci

Many people struggle to achieve because they're not ambitious. Being ambitious may stir your fears—fear of success, failure, regret, disappointment, or loss. Or it may trigger a fear of standing out. You may associate ambition with negative traits, like aggression.

Reframe ambition and look to your heroes and heroines. As Leonardo once said, "I want to create miracles." If that's not ambitious I don't know what is. He wasn't hard and aggressive—he was focused on escaping the fires of mediocrity and he kept his vision fixed on success.

YOUR CHALLENGE

When you think of someone ambitious that you admire who comes to mind?

What qualities do they possess? How could you copy-cat or borrow these qualities and apply them to help you succeed?

Keep your ambition a secret—avoid the critics and those who may knock your confidence. When you start to flap your ambition wings other people may feel threatened or jealous

It's cool to be ambitious. People want to hang out with ambitious, successful people. Pursue your big audacious goals! Do the things you think you can't. Achieve the impossible.

Read more tips to stimulate your ambition on my blog.

The world is in perpetual motion, and we must invent the things of tomorrow. One must go before others, be determined and exacting, and let your intelligence direct your life. Act with audacity .

~ Madame Veuve Cliquot, businesswoman

PLAN FOR SUCCESS

*God sells us all things
at the price of labor.*

~ Leonardo da Vinci

Planning and effort prevents poor performance. This is such a powerful message when it comes to our goals, especially if you're someone who equates planning with feeling controlled. You may be looking to the future thinking, "Someday! Someday I will achieve that."

How can you be assured that things will happen if you don't plan your action steps effectively, efficiently and productively?

So many people end their lives disappointed that things didn't come to fruition. "Why didn't it happen for me? Why, when it happens for other people." Successful people don't sit at home waiting for things to happen. They go out and conquer things.

If you're sitting back waiting for 'someday' you have a problem—you think you have time!

YOUR CHALLENGE

Set one goal for yourself and start breaking it down into bite size chunks. If you want to generate $100,000 out of your business in a year what do you need to do to get there?

If you want to start a new relationship, or improve the one you've got, develop your success strategy. Your efforts will be repaid in exchange for your labor and your courage to try.

Do the one thing you think you cannot do. Fail at it. Try again. Do better the second time. The only people who never tumble are those who never mount the high wire. This is your moment. Own it.

~ Oprah, businesswoman

BE SOLUTION-FOCUSED

Look at the light and consider its beauty. Blink your eye and look at it again: what you see was not there at first, and what was there is no more.

~ Leonardo da Vinci

One of the most common questions people who answered The Art of Success questionnaire said they would ask both Leonardo da Vinci and I—is how do we keep going in the face of obstacles? What gives us persistence?

One of the essential things is believing your goal or dream is worth fighting for. Do you want it bad enough? Does it fill your soul with fire? Without passion in your heart you won't have energy, making it hard to get started—let alone to keep going.

But even with fire in your soul, you need to fan the flames of desire with a healthy dose of optimism, and lavish doses of self-soothing, in the face of setbacks.

I'm just like you. I feel defeated sometimes. Worn out. Frustrated. And sometimes I wonder if it's all just too hard. Leonardo did too.

Sometimes we have no idea how to overcome the obstacles we face. But—after allowing ourselves to feel natural emotions such as despondency, frustration, and despair—we must get on with generating solutions.

Leonardo loved solving problems. He thrived on challenge. He didn't like anything getting the better of him. And he loved to succeed—qualities you can cultivate.

YOUR CHALLENGE

Go on a problem-free diet. Talk and proactively look for solutions

Feeling fearful? Feel the fear and act 'as if' you are confident, courageous and full of massive self-belief

I don't think of myself as a poor deprived ghetto girl who made good. I think of myself as somebody who from an early age knew I was responsible for myself, and I had to make good.

~ Oprah Winfrey, businesswoman

PRINCIPLE THREE: EMPOWER YOUR VISION

BEGIN WITH THE END IN SIGHT

There are three classes of people: those who see. Those who see when they are shown. Those who do not see.

~ Leonardo da Vinci

"He is thinking of the end before he has begun the work," complained Pope Leo X. "This man will do nothing at all!"

Pope Leo X, born Giovanni di Lorenzo de' Medici, had commissioned a painting and was vexed to see that Leonardo began by distilling certain herbs and oils to create a new form of varnish to put over the artwork when completed.

Yet as Stephen Covey made famous in his influential book, *The Seven Habits of Highly Successful People,* beginning with the end in mind (seeing the project completed) and sharpening the saw (preparing your tools of success) are important preparatory steps, steps that people impatient for results often neglect.

Beginning with the end in sight, is also a powerful way of strengthening motivation, persistence and perseverance. The future does belong to those believe in the beauty of their dreams and schemes

YOUR CHALLENGE

Let desire propel you forward by acting as if, seeing as if, feeling as if, tasting as if, touching as if your success has already been achieved.

- You attract the things you think about—out of sight, out of mind. Here's a few ways to keep your goals in sight:
- Visualize your preferred future. Create a vision, success, or manifestation collage—or do as I once did and create a manifestation fridge
- Borrow from your ultimate future. Remind yourself daily of the benefits success will bring
- A year from now where do you want to be? Looking back, if you had started one year ago where would you be today? It's not too late to start.

DON'T BE DISHEARTENED or discouraged if other people can't see what you can see, or they don't believe in your vision. If you can see it, and you can believe it, in time you can achieve it.

When you take a flower in your hand and really look at it, it's your world for the moment. I want to give that world to someone else. Most people in the city rush around so, they have no time to look at a flower. I want them to see it whether they want to or not.

~ Georgia O'Keeffe, artist

JOURNAL

*Dimmi—tell me...tell me whether...
tell me how things are...tell me if there was ever.*

~ Leonardo da Vinci

History has been made richer by the many successful men and women who kept daily journals. Marcus Aurelius, Benjamin Franklin, and Julia Cameron, playwright and author of phenomenal bestseller *The Artist's Way*, all understand the transformational power of journals. As did Leonardo.

He was a prolific recorder of all things that interested and excited him. He maintained over 13,000 pages of scientific notes and drawings on natural philosophy, life, travel and mysteries.

"Preserve these sketches as your assistants and masters," he once wrote in his journal.

His notebooks not only log his interests and the things he witnessed with his own eyes, but it was also a medium by which he channelled his intuition. His journals further evidence his belief in the existence of universal knowledge and divine intelligence.

He habitually doodled the word 'dimmi' which translates 'tell me', or 'speak to me', asking for answers and by posing questions. Today we commonly refer to this as seeking intuitive insight.

Journalling helped Leonardo clarify his thinking, affirm his goals, make sense of everything, understand, learn, and grow.

His journals supported him throughout his life—helping him overcome doubts and fears and achieve self-mastery.

YOUR CHALLENGE

How can your journals be both servant and master in the journey to success?

Do you already have a journal? Do you record the present and dream of the future. Have you made journalling a daily habit?

Write what should not be forgotten.

~ Isabel Allende, author

THE ART OF SUCCESS

Art is the queen of all sciences communicating knowledge to all the generations of the world.

~ Leonardo da Vinci

After enduring years of disappointment, losses and failures, and following the shunning of his work by Pope Leo X in Rome, Leonardo left Italy. Taking one of his most famous paintings with him—the portrait of Mona Lisa—he took up residence with Francis I, the King of France.

The power of exceptional works of heart transcend the rational mind. They transcend time and space. They immortalize knowledge that sustains, empowers, encourages and inspires.

Leonardo refused to be parted from his portrait of Mona Lisa. She was his queen—embodying and communicating the knowledge he valued most.

Many people underestimate the power of art. But it's not lost on the wealthy and successful who surround themselves with quality pieces.

But art needn't be expensive to work its magic. You don't need to even own it.

"Art is how spirit speaks to you," a psychic once told me. And it's true. It's the reason I began writing my historical novel *Mona Lisa's Secret*.

It's also the reason I persevered despite feeling overwhelmed by the enormity and responsibility of tackling writing about such an iconic painting.

One day, after a lengthy period of giving in to resistance, while visiting an exhibition of Renaissance paintings a portrait of a young nun spoke to me, "What are you waiting for," she challenged. "You're not like me. You have your liberty. You have choice."

YOUR CHALLENGE

What visual cue or icon can you carry with you to power your success and embody the truths and values you cherish most?

How does it speak to you?

> *We do not judge great art.*
> *It judges us.*
>
> ~ Caroline Herschel, astronomer

BRAINSTORM IDEAS

By indistinct things the mind is stimulated to new inventions.

~ Leonardo da Vinci

Are you lost for ideas? As Martin Kemp notes in *The Marvellous Works of Nature and Man*, the foundation of many of Leonardo's greatest works began in a 'brainstorm' of dynamic sketching, scribbled in a frenzy of creative impatience.

Letting go of rigidly planning, and in its place allowing ideas to flow with the flexibility of preparatory sketching became the norm for later centuries.

But it was introduced almost single-handedly by Leonardo. Many of his ideas and inventions were triggered by looking for patterns, meaning and significance in seemingly unrelated ideas or objects.

Leonardo once wrote, "Do not despise my opinion, when I remind you that it should not be hard for you to stop sometimes and look into the stains of walls, or the ashes of a fire, or clouds, or mud or like places, in which, if you consider them well, you may find really marvelous ideas…*because by indistinct things the mind is stimulated to new inventions."*

When I was at architecture school took a class teaching furniture design. My tutor, frustrated by my linear and rational thinking, encouraged me to pair insects with tables to generate more interesting designs. My mind expanded—suddenly a table no longer needed to be square and have four legs!

YOUR CHALLENGE

Whenever you feel blocked, lost for ideas, or don't know about how to proceed, brainstorm. Set the timer for three minutes, or longer, and mind map your way to success by generating a range of possible solutions. Intensify the impact by encouraging supportive others to brainstorm ideas too.

Ask open generative questions to increase your range of options, "*how, what, where, what else*" etc., and combine different ideas to open your mind to new ideas and possibilities.

Don't close down any 'crazy' ideas prematurely.

I don't want to be seen as an outsider necessarily, but it means I can carry on with experimentation and innovation.

~ Dame Zaha Mohammad Hadid, architect

FANTASIA

Science is the observation of things possible, whether present or past. Prescience is the knowledge of things that may come to pass, though but slowly.

~ Leonardo da Vinci

What do you ask first? What's realistic? Or what's possible? So many people want guarantees of success before taking action. But Leonardo's success was primarily driven by his deep and fertile imagination—or what he termed *fantasia*. Fantasia he believed, was a core requirement for a successful creator.

He fed his imagination with a diversity of sources. Records kept from his book lists showed that he owned chivalric romances, imaginative poetry, collections of tales, fables and jests, as well, as scientific and fact-based texts.

To succeed, you need to establish a union between *the intelletto*, rational understanding, and *fantasia*, imaginative composition.

But in the beginning give yourself permission to let your mind, and spirit soar. Don't get bogged down by limited rational thinking. This will stifle creativity, and narrow your capacity for out-of-the-orbit thinking.

Numerous scientific studies show that novelty and 'weird' experiences stimulate creativity. Imagine, as Leonardo did, impossible things. Daydream. Create or read about absurd things.

YOUR CHALLENGE

How can you create more fantastical ideas?

What's impossible? What if it were possible? How could you make it come true? How would your future be different?

Believe in the fantastic.

~ Dame Zaha Mohammad Hadid, architect

LEAD DON'T FOLLOW

Once you have tasted flight, you will forever walk the earth with your eyes turned skyward, for there you have been, and there you will always long to return.

~ Leonardo da Vinci

Leonardo combined what he loved with his vision and talent for fulfilling future needs. The threat of war made him design things that would protect cities. The desire for faster travel propelled his quest to find a way for man to fly. Illness and death drove him to understand the human body.

He once said, "The painter will produce pictures of little merit if he takes the works of others as his standard."

His creations were original, and many artists of the time copied him—including Raphael. Many of Leonardo's designs were spectacularly ahead of his time.

So many of his ideas were impossible to build during the 15th and 16th centuries with the tools available and Leonardo's financial constraints. However 500-plus years later he's still regarded as a leader.

YOUR CHALLENGE

Don't chase the market. Create a need, or fulfill anticipated ones. Don't be deterred if at first you don't succeed. Do what you dream about and wait for the world to catch up. No one really knows what, or who, be the next hot thing.

Persevere with your vision. Let the beauty and imagineering you love be the work that you do. Cocoon yourself in the protective magic and power of creative, lateral, blue-skies thinking.

Read and learn about other leaders and pioneers. And become the lead character in your own book of life.

You are the storyteller of your own life, and you can create your own legend, or not.

~ Isabel Allende, author

PUT YOUR WEIGHT INTO YOUR DREAMS

A man will always, involuntarily, throw the greater weight towards the point whither he desires to move than in any other direction.

~ Leonardo da Vinci

It's pretty hard to gain any traction when your heart is not engaged. Whether you're just starting out on your quest for success, or facing a mountain of obstacles, it's imperative to put your weight into your dreams.

Leonardo threw his mind, body and soul into his deepest desires. When he became obsessed with mathematics and sacred geometry this became his focus, with some people complaining he had stopped painting and 'had little time for the brush.'

When understanding the human body became central the weight of his considerable mind was channeled into figuring out its workings.

When you truly commit, mind, body and soul you'll engage the laws of physics and move forwards with incredible velocity.

YOUR CHALLENGE

How whole-hearted are you?

Do you have one foot in the door and the other foot out?

What would it take to strengthen your desire?

Put your weight into your dreams but keep an eye on the day-to-day realities that sustain you.

> *The biggest adventure you can take*
> *is to live the life of your dreams.*

~ Oprah, businesswoman

FOCUS

The mind that engages in subjects of too great variety becomes confused and weakened.

~ Leonardo da Vinci

There are divergent thoughts on what it means to be focused. Some people believe you focus on only one thing, one task, one priority at the time. Only when you have finished that task do you move to the next. Great! If that works for you, you have your success strategy.

But some people like Leonardo da Vinci thrive on variety. Seeing one thing through to the end often bored him—stifling his creativity and productivity.

Leonardo also disproves the myth that you can't have more than one passion to be successful. He was passionate about so many things—beauty, nature, science, human behavior, nature, architecture, the human body, sacred geometry, the soul…and more.

However look closely and you'll see a central unifying theme—the attempt to replicate nature's beauty and power, and the acquisition of knowledge born from his own experience.

He described himself as many things, but tellingly he once said he was simply an inventor. He acquired knowledge to see what more he could do with it.

YOUR CHALLENGE

If a lack of focus is something getting in your way, really drill down into the causal factors. Play the role of scientist. Discover the cause, identify the effect, hypothesize solutions, and experiment until you find a strategy that works. Perhaps the issue is less about focus and more about self-discipline!

Eckhart Tole, author of *The Power of Now*, advocates surrender. Whatever is holding your attention now—surrender to it. Focus on what you 'should' be doing at a later date

Juggling too many balls? Prioritize them, set a timer, and allocate segmented time for all the competing activities you feel must get done.

Practise creative procrastination. Ask yourself, "What is the best use of my time right now?" Put off everything else.

Remind yourself of a time when you struggled to focus. What worked then that you could apply now?

The Universe has a wonderful way of self-correcting once you get out of your own way.

In our daily lives, moving from struggle to grace requires practice and commitment.

~ Arianna Huffington, businesswoman

TAKE ACTION

It had long since come to my attention that people of accomplishment rarely sat back and let things happen to them. They went out and happened to things.

~ Leonardo da Vinci

Do you have an action, 'make things happen' mindset, or do you believe in luck, serendipity, going with the flow, or waiting for opportunities to find you?

So many people take a passive route when it comes to achieving their goals. Others wait until all the stars are aligned. Not Leonardo, and hopefully not you!

Despite being criticized for not finishing everything he started, when Leonardo wanted to achieve something, he visualized the end goal, and did what he needed to do to make his vision a reality.

When Leonardo needed a new patron—one with power and deep pockets—he didn't sit back. Sometimes he faked it until he made it by talking up his successes.

When he 'cold-called' Ludovico Sforza, the then de facto ruler of Milan, seeking employment he talked-up his achievements.

Fully aware that Sforza was looking to employ military engineers, Leonardo drafted an application letter emphasizing engineering talents and skills he had yet to fully develop, and assuring the Duke of his ability to achieve impossible feats.

Leonardo got the job!

YOUR CHALLENGE

Do you plan your life by:

- Beginning with the end in mind—planning at least five to ten years ahead, and working back from there to ensure that everything you do now moves you ahead?
- Creating outcome-focused goals?
- Or do you get bogged down in rigidly planning every minute step you have to make to achieve the changes—instead of trusting you will figure it, or trusting the Universe or providence to deliver?

It's a balancing act! Whatever your approach, pledge to make your success a reality. Act as if who and what you desire to be is already a reality.

Luck is preparation meeting opportunity.

~ Oprah, businesswoman

GROUND YOUR VISION

The earth has a spirit of growth.

~ Leonardo da Vinci

Leonardo's visions came from the skies and realms above; the implementation of his ideas from the earth below. To achieve success he knew he needed to ground himself. He new he had to come from a place of earthy strength and stillness.

Sometimes during the visionary process your mind may race, as Leonardo's did, with wild, unbridled excitement about all the possibilities. Or perhaps, your mind may drum with anxiety. Unstructured energy can pull you in different directions, overwhelming or immobilizing you.

Ground your vision and prepare to engage your analytical mind, you'll have better judgement, clarity of thinking and more self-assured energy.

YOUR CHALLENGE

Re-organize yourself. Touch base with what's real., what's practical, what needs to be done. Ground your vision by identifying the body of work you'll need to complete to make your ideas tangible.

Defrag your visionary mind. Take your shoes off and connect with the earth. Step away from technology. Spend time quietly in nature, as Leonardo often did, listen to Her whispers. Notebook in hand, allow your intuition to guide you.

When you're feeling grounded set about gathering and analyzing information, designing and testing solutions to problems, and formulating plans. This can still be done creatively.

For example, you may wish to:

- Name all the tangible seeds you need to plant
- Identify the optimal planting conditions that will allow your ideas to sprout
- Weed out any inner blocks, limiting beliefs, assumptions or mind-chatter that may keep you from taking positive action.
- Prepare your planting plan
- Go plant!

If you're a list maker—you know what to do!

*Facilitate the translation of principles
into explicit practical forms.*

~ Ada Lovelace, mathematician

PRINCIPLE FOUR: EMPOWER YOUR SPIRIT

WORSHIP THE GOD WITHIN

The definition of the soul I leave to the imaginations of friars, those fathers of the people who know all secrets by inspiration. I leave alone the sacred books; for they are supreme truth.

~ Leonardo da Vinci

Rumors abound about Leonardo's beliefs, but one thing is certain, he was not blind to the failings, corruption and hypocrisy of the men who claimed to represent God on earth.

The Medici and Borgias, members of the ruling classes during the Renaissance, rose to be clerics and popes. Historical records confirm they were motivated by their own pursuit of power and pleasure more than the salvation of others.

They also actively censored the cultivation of beliefs which threatened their own power base.

Leonardo was also aware of men altering and rewriting ancient biblical texts—including the zealous Dominican priest Savonarola, who also burned thousands of beautiful artworks and musical instruments he regarded as sinful vanities.

But spirituality and faith, as it is for so many people, was important to Leonardo's success. Not just because so many of his commissions were from the church, but because he believed in the power of God, divinity and soul.

Rather than subscribe to dogma Leonardo found his strength and grounded his faith in roots that can be traced to ancient Gnosticism and Neoplatonism.

Gnostic ideas influenced many ancient religions and believed that gnosis—interpreted as knowledge, enlightenment 'oneness with God, the divine creator—could be accessed directly. Searching for wisdom by helpful others led to direct communion with God—no third party intermediary such as a pope or priest required.

Many of Leonardo's Christian-based religious paintings are said to 'hide in plain sight' Leonardo's deepest beliefs, and rebellious thinking, which if more strongly asserted would have been called heresy.

Deepak Chopra writes in *The Seven Spiritual Laws of Success*, once you learn to live in harmony with natural law, a sense of well-being, good health, fulfilling relationships, energy and enthusiasm for life and material abundance will spring forth easily and effortlessly.

Some of many benefits Leonardo gained from worshipping the god within include:

- Access to divine wisdom
- A deep connection with universal knowledge
- Faith, hope and strength during testing times
- A guiding sense of purpose

YOUR CHALLENGE

What does spirituality mean to you?

What spiritual beliefs and practices sustain and empower you?

If spirituality is not something you believe in examine your beliefs. Why? Why not? What mistaken beliefs might you have absorbed?

While many people have found comfort in religion, others have had traumatic experiences. Examine how religion and spirituality are the same and how they differ.

> *He who has a mind to understand,*
> *let him understand.*
>
> ~ Mary Magdalene, in The Gospel of Mary

BE AN OUTLIER

*I awoke, only to find the rest
of the world was still asleep.*

~ Leonardo da Vinci

Too often people are afraid to stand out from the crowd. Often the innovative path is the path less followed but, as actress Drew Barrymore says, "Originality is believing in your individuality, believing in yourself, and being willing to take risks, even though people might think you're weird for doing it."

Yet so many people seek, and then struggle, to fit in with the 'norm.' But not Leonardo da Vinci—he was one of the greatest and most successful outliers of all.

He was a free-thinker, unbounded by convention. He was motivated by his own search for truth born from his own experience—not the dogma of others.

So many people are sleeping through their lives. Leonardo was awake, shining the light on truth, advancement, the progress of humanity.

Only in recent years have engineers begun to construct his amazing designs. Were it not for his curiosity and willingness to stand out from the crowd Leonardo da Vinci would have faded into obscurity.

YOUR CHALLENGE

Are you prepared to stand out from the crowd and live a significant life?

What do you need to start, stop, do more of or less of to be a confident outlier?

I don't really feel I'm part of the establishment. I'm not outside, I'm on the kind of edge, I'm dangling there. I quite like it ... I'm not against the establishment per se. I just do what I do and that's it.

~ Dame Zaha Mohammad Hadid, architect

DEVOTE YOURSELF

A life without love, is no life at all.

- Leonardo da Vinci

Success without love is no success at all. A life dedicated to what inspires you, that fills you with joy and gives you passion and fulfillment is a life truly lived. The French call this your métier.

Others, like author Deepak Chopra call this your dharma, or purpose in life. Joy, bliss—call it what you will—you'll know it when you feel it.

On my business card I have the following quote by the ancient philosopher Sophocles, "One word frees us from the weight and pain of life: That word is love."

Love is such a power antidote to all that troubles us—it's the Swiss Army knife of all things healing.

My passion, purpose, and inspiration is simple—love. I love to bring more love into the world. I know that love is a contagious energy—when I am inspired my love spreads love into the world.

Leonardo's inspiration? Nature. He sought to both understand and replicate Her beauty and her wisdom—and in doing so, to bring more love into existence.

Love is the highest, most powerful vibration on earth. It radiates light, driving out darkness. When you work with love people feel it. It permeates everything you do and draws people who are attracted by the power of this energy to you.

YOUR CHALLENGE

Wed yourself, as Leonardo did, to the experiences that awaken your heart.

What or who do you love with such a passion you will devote your life to it?

> *Heart is what drives us and determines our fate.*
>
> ~ Isabel Allende, author

FOLLOW your passion and purpose to prosperity—online coaching program

If you need more help to find and live your life purpose you may prefer to take my online course, and watch inspirational and practical videos and other strategies to help you to fulfill your potential.

Click here to enroll or find out more—the-coaching-lab.teachable.com/p/follow-your-passion-and-purpose-to-prosperity

INTEGRATE YOUR MIND, BODY AND SOUL

All knowledge has its origins in our perceptions.

~ Leonardo da Vinci

Thinking and feeling, heart versus head, mind versus body, have played a dual battle for supremacy throughout history as the centre for knowledge.

Yet in truth neither is supreme. The power you give to one over the other is only in your perceptions.

However, many people believe that love, awe, wonder, worship—and success, in particular—depends on the integration of your mind, body and soul. For balance, all must work as one.

Leonardo was fascinated with how the heart functioned, but also the pineal gland, a small structure about the size of a pea, located in the middle of the brain.

He believed, as René Descartes, a French philosopher, mathematician, and scientist, that the pineal gland was where the soul attached to the body and passion resided. Accessing this tiny gland, he and other modern-day scientists believe, provides a direct channel to higher wisdom and divine intelligence.

Perhaps this was how Leonardo was able to so accurately predict the future.

YOUR CHALLENGE

Access this higher knowledge by adopting some of the following spiritual practices:

- Meditating
- Journaling
- Following your passions
- Surrounding yourself with like-minded people
- Immersing yourself in nature
- Accessing your sub-conscious and super-conscious minds
- Retreating into solitude
- Reading sacred books and accessing ancients' knowledge of the spiritual realms
- Consulting the Akashic Records, or "Hall of Knowledge. (I invite you to contact me for a personalized reading).

Honor the mind-body and spiritual dimension. When your spirit is off-centre, the odds are your work and relationships will be too.

> *O admirable necessity!*
> *O powerful action!*
> *What mind can penetrate your nature?*
> *What language can express this marvel?*
> *None, to be sure.*
> *This is where human discourse*
> *turns toward the contemplation of the divine.*
>
> ~ Leonardo da Vinci

WORK WITH SPIRIT

Where the spirit does not work with the hand, there is no art.

~ Leonardo da Vinci

If your soul is not in your work, there is no heart. Without heart your work lacks passion, purpose and power.

These are all sources of energy and the key to the authenticity people love. People can spot a fake. Fakes and frauds lack conviction, energy and vitality.

Oprah once said, "I am not successful because of luck. I am successful because I paid attention." She also said, "I wish I'd known be authentic would make me so much money."

Discovering, honoring and sharing your gifts and working with your soul purpose is to work with spirit.

YOUR CHALLENGE

Pay attention to what fills your soul with fire.

Pay attention to what's real for you.

Pay attention when your spirit feels suffocated.

Whatever you put your hand to, imbue it with the spirit of love.

Passion is energy. Feel the power that comes from focusing on what excites you. You know you are on the road to success if you would do your job, and not be paid for it.

~ Oprah, businesswoman

SHOW UP

I have been impressed with the urgency of doing. Knowing is not enough: we must apply. Being willing is not enough; we must do.

~ Leonardo da Vinci

To be inspired is to be in spirit, and inspiration has to find you working or it won't come out to play. Eighty percent of success is empowering your mind, body and spirit by showing up.

Showing up requires the ability to balance creativity with flexibility and discipline.

To be disciplined is to be committed, devoted, able to control your Self in accordance with, and sometimes against, your desires.

You may be a genius, gifted or have an IQ of 160, but if you lack self-discipline and follow through your success will be limited.

Leonardo affirmed the importance of this by writing reminders to himself of the superiority of doing to knowing. Like two very gifted dance partners, one must lead.

CASSANDRA GAISFORD

YOUR CHALLENGE

How can you create a sense of urgency and show up?

What do you need to start, stop, do more of, or less of?

> *Show up. Show up.*
> *When you show up the muse shows up, too.*
>
> ~ Isabel Allende, author

FIND YOUR SACRED SPACE

Men of lofty genius when they are doing the least work are most active.

~ Leonardo da Vinci

Finding your sacred space—a place where you can retreat from the world, contemplate, and reflect, and just take time out from your overloaded conscious mind, is an important part of connecting with your higher self and inner wisdom.

Being in nature was one of Leonardo's favorite sacred spaces. Perhaps it's yours too. Maybe your sacred space is a favorite room, a garden shed or some other place where you can have uninterrupted time.

Your sacred space may be amongst other like-minded people, perhaps a spiritual place of worship or a meditation retreat. Or even a place where you can indulge your passions and joys. Doing something you love is often a meditation in itself.

Resist setting an agenda or specific expectations. Go with nothing more than to dedicate yourself to nurturing the divine within. Nourish your soul and watch your spirit and capacity for greatness soar.

CASSANDRA GAISFORD

YOUR CHALLENGE

Where is your sacred space?

If you don't have one make finding it a priority.

My bedroom is my sanctuary. It's like a refuge, and it's where I do a fair amount of designing—at least conceptually, if not literally.

~ Vera Wang, fashion designer

THE SACREDNESS OF NUMBERS

No human investigation can be called real science if it cannot be demonstrated mathematically.

~ Leonardo Da Vinci

You may believe in lucky numbers or you may call it superstition but Leonardo revered the science and sacred mysteries of mathematical proportion.

His curiosity piqued he devoted many years to understanding and applying the ancient knowledge of sacred geometry.

Why sacred? Sacred geometry involves sacred universal patterns which appear and are used in the design in *everything* in our reality.

The whole of the Universe is said to be contained within a grain of sand. The mysteries of science, mathematics and the higher heavens can be found in naturally recurring patterns of numbers which link man, animals, nature and the Universe.

Guided by the sacredness of numbers and divine proportion some of the world's most enduring sacred monuments dedicated to worship, beauty, and excellence have been created—including Egypt's Great Pyramids, and Florence's magnificent Cathedral of Santa Maria del Fiore.

Geometry and mathematical ratios, harmonics and proportions are also found in some of the world's most captivating art works, including Leonardo's Last Supper and the Mona Lisa. They're also found in light, cosmology and music.

So powerful are these forms, they are believed by many to enable you to commune directly with The Divine (God or Source), rather than requiring intermediaries such as a priest.

Coco Chanel, (the inspiration for the second book in *Anxiety Rescue* series), believed so strongly in the power of the number five she named her perfume Chanel No5.

Taught the precepts of theosophy by one of her lovers, she knew the numerological significance of it, as representative of the fifth element —the legendary *quinta essentia* of the alchemists, the Classical quintessence of which it is believed by many the cosmos is made.

"I'm presenting my dress collection on the 5th of May, the fifth month of the year," she once said.

YOUR CHALLENGE

What numbers are harmonious to you?

What are your success numbers?

Look deeper into the world of numbers and proportion and discover their secret mysteries.

> *If you find from your own experience that something is a fact and it contradicts what some authority has written down, then you must abandon the authority and base your reasoning on your own findings.*
>
> ~ Leonardo da Vinci

PRINCIPLE FIVE: EMPOWER YOUR MIND

CULTIVATE A SUCCESS MINDSET

*You cannot help being good,
because your hand and your mind,
being accustomed to gather flowers
would ill know how to pluck thorns.*

~ Leonardo da Vinci

His Holiness the 14th Dalai Lama once said, "Negative thoughts are like weeds, but positive thoughts are like flowers—they need nurturing every day."

Leonardo proactively fertilized his mind, and empowered his resolve by focusing on his dreams, goals and aspirations.

To steady himself against self-doubt or the attacks of others he actively cultivated a success mindset by using affirmations, journaling, meditating, channeling and accessing the spiritual realms, and surrounding himself with like-minded, aspirational and inspirational people.

If you actively cultivate a success mindset you cannot help being good, because your mind, focused on the fruits of your positive intention and effort will act as a barrier to discouragement, keeping away the thorns of self-doubt, procrastination, fear or any of the other things toxic to your success.

YOUR CHALLENGE

Attitude is everything. How can you cultivate a success mindset?

> *Think like a queen. A queen is not afraid to fail. Failure is another stepping stone to greatness.*
>
> ~ Oprah, businesswoman

MOTIVATE YOURSELF

You will never have a greater or lesser dominion than that over yourself...the height of a man's success is gauged by his self-mastery; the depth of his failure by his self-abandonment.

~ Leonardo da Vinci

To succeed in life you need to master yourself, assume the command position, take control and motivate yourself. Whether you need to master new technical skills or master the art of self-discipline, when you fail to be the boss of you, you are giving away your power.

Leonardo once said that people were more motivated by fear than they were love. Desperation can be a wonderful motivator. But so can love.

Whether you're fueled by the carrot or the whip your job is to produce your work to a special level, in a specific amount of time, in order to create the life you desire. No excuses.

Whether your motivation is intrinsic—the rewards that come from doing the work itself; or extrinsic—external rewards such as money or status, the questions you ask can be powerful catalysts to inspired action. The art lies in crafting questions that get better outcomes.

YOUR CHALLENGE

Instead of saying, "How can I be more self-disciplined?" asking, "How can I master the art of self-motivation and discipline and have fun doing it?" may yield better results.

Similarly, instead of saying, "How can I be more successful?" try asking "How can I be more successful and have a blast doing it?" Listen for the answers and then take action.

Stephen Covey, author of *The 7 Habits of Highly Effective People*, says the ability to subordinate an impulse to a value is the essence of the proactive person.

What do you value? Fulfillment? Freedom? Joy? Continuous learning? Achieving a worthwhile goal? High earnings? Achieving your potential? Completion? Or something else? Often the things you struggle against reveal your values most

Reaffirm your success values to empower your success.

Where there is no struggle,
there is no strength.

~ Oprah, businesswoman

OVERCOME PROCRASTINATION

Inaction saps the vigors of the mind.

~ Leonardo da Vinci

Leonardo once wrote in his journal, "It is easier to resist at the beginning than at the end."

This simple statement is a reminder of what we all know to be true—getting started is often the most difficult part of taking inspired action.

The result is almost always procrastination—the great robber of time, talent and potential.

But it's an easy thief to tame if you keep your mind focused on your end goal and just do it. Once you get started your mind and spirit will become instantly invigorated.

YOUR CHALLENGE

Do you want success badly enough to just do the things that need to be done—NOW?

What disempowering beliefs, attitudes or habits are holding you back? Dig deep. Unearth the culprits.

Recall a time in the past when you procrastinated. What was your success strategy?

Whip procrastination into shape by taking inspired action. Set the timer for five minutes and see how much harder it is to stop once you've started.

I made a conscious decision not to stop.

~ Dame Zaha Mohammad Hadid, architect

CULTIVATE HOPE

One's thoughts turn towards Hope.

~ Leonardo da Vinci

Common obstacles to success include fear, self-doubt, anxiety, and other crippling thoughts. But what if all you had to do to tame these uglies was cultivate hope?

The power of hope is grounded firmly in spiritual and religious practices but also in science. Like the ancient Greeks and Romans, Leonardo da Vinci, and even 18th century physicians, recognized the physiological effects of mind-power and hope on the body.

Successful medical outcomes, even when the intervention is a placebo, further evidence the impact of maintaining a positive expectation.

If like me, you've manifested miracles in your own life, by maintaining a positive expectation, you'll know the power of hope.

Thoughts *do* become things. Scientists Gregg Braden and also Bruce Lipton, author of *The Biology of Belief,* have evidenced this.

But hope can only flourish when you believe that what you do can make a difference, that you recognize that you have choices, and that your actions can create a future which differs from your present situation.

When you empower your belief in your ability to gain some control over your circumstances, you are no longer entirely at the mercy of forces outside yourself. You are back in the driving seat.

What you believe has a tremendous influence on the likelihood of success. Reframe your fears and buoy your dreams with hope. Not, "I'm afraid of failing" but "I hope to succeed," or something similar.

YOUR CHALLENGE

How could you cultivate more hope?

Fearlessness is like a muscle.
I know from my own life
that the more I exercise it
the more natural it becomes
to not let my fears run me.

~ Arianna Huffington, businesswomen

ALLOW NO DOUBT

Obstacles cannot crush me;
every obstacle yields to stern resolve.

~ Leonardo da Vinci

Attitude is everything. Be a guard for your words, thoughts and feelings. Don't let self-doubt be the thing that deflates you.

Winners like Leonardo da Vinci are too busy to be sad, too positive to be doubtful, too optimistic to be fearful, too focused on success and too determined to be defeated.

Be your biggest fan. Back yourself 100 percent. We all have doubts, but it's amazing how your doubts will disappear once you're doing the things you love.

As you've already read, Leonardo cultivated hope, visualized the end goal, used affirmations, and studious effort to slay his doubt demons.

He also backed his ideas and saw failure as a normal and often necessary part of success.

YOUR CHALLENGE

Are you your biggest fan or worst enemy? How can you stay positive, confident and optimistic?

You will need the confidence to take new steps every time; hard work will give you that layer of confidence.

~ Dame Zaha Mohammad Hadid, architect

DON'T LET THE CRITICS STOP YOU

*The greatest deception men suffer
is from their own opinions.*

~ Leonardo da Vinci

Listening too much to others, or overly seeking validation and approval, can really hinder your success. If you try to please everyone you'll never succeed.

Plenty of successful people have received scathing reviews, rejections and public humiliation from peers and critics but they persevered with their vision anyway.

You'll know some of the more famous ones. Author J.K Rowling's *Harry Potter* series was rejected many times by publishers who told her that there wasn't a big market for books targeted at children.

The singer Meatloaf was told that he was too fat to make it big and no one would want to see a 'weird' performance like *Bat Out of Hell*.

Film producer Peter Jackson was cautioned to stay away from a trilogy and make *The Lord of the Rings* into one normal length movie.

Yet these men and women, and others like them, stayed true to their quest. And they all went on to be colossal successes.

Other people may believe their criticisms of you, your ideas, your work. But what if they are wrong? What if your vision, like Leonardo Da Vinci's was back in the 1500's, is way ahead of its time?

Sometimes feedback is helpful. But not if it stops you in your tracks or you are so consumed with garnering everyone's approval you become immobilized.

Nobody can stop you but you. You have to ignore your harshest critics. To thy self you must remain true. Imagine how many of Leonardo's ideas would never have come to fruition if he'd listened to others.

YOUR CHALLENGE

Forge ahead. Blaze your road to success with your victories—even if the victory is just the one you win over your self-doubt, your laziness, your procrastination, your thoughts that you have no talent, or some other self-defeating chatter.

What's worse—the disappointment of criticism and bad reviews, or the bitter, bitter disappointment of a life spent unfulfilled and filled with regret?

All life arises out of choice. What choices are you making now?

How can you stay strong in the wake of criticism?

How can you do more of what's working for you, and less of what's not? What can you start and stop doing to boost your chances of success?

No one ever truly knows what the market will do next, nor the music you hold inside!

TOO MANY PEOPLE die with regret . . . far better to say at least you tried . . . and even better, that you kept going. Trust yourself and believe in your work!

> *It's not 'What do I want to do?'*
> *It's 'What kind of life do I want to have?'*
>
> ~ Arianna Huffington, businesswoman

MAINTAIN SOME BALANCE

Every now and then go away, have a little relaxation, for when you come back to your work your judgment will be surer. Go some distance away because then the work appears smaller and more of it can be taken in at a glance and a lack of harmony and proportion is more readily seen.

~ Leonardo da Vinci

Workaholism is an addiction for many passionate people. Others use overwork to medicate their unhappiness in other areas of their life—most commonly dissatisfaction with their relationships.

When you work slavishly, particularly at something you love, your brain releases chemicals called opiates which create feelings of euphoria. No wonder it's hard to step away!

Euphoria stems from the Greek word *euphoría*—the power of enduring easily. But consider what the state of endurance implies. Enduring implies force or strain, or gritting your teeth and bearing it at times. Force or strain with no respite leads to stress, robbing you of vital energy.

Many people find when they don't step away from their work they suffer disillusionment, and things that once filled them with passion no longer fill them with joy. Resentment builds and relationships with family, friends etc. can suffer.

Addictively working offers a short-term fix, but lasting happiness needs variety—and nourishment. Being with family or friends, engaging in a hobby, spending time in nature, learning something new, helping others, or just being solitary will help you avoid burnout, nourish your brain, heart and soul, improve your judgement and restore harmony.

To be truly happy and successful you must be able to be at peace when you are working and when you are at rest.

Leonardo would often take breaks from his work to refresh his mind and spirit. While others claimed he took too long to finish things he knew the importance of replenishing his focus to maintain a clear perspective.

He also valued sleep, noting in one of his journals that some of his best insights came when his mind was not working.

Even if you love the work that you do it is fun to get away from it and have objective-free time, space to unwind and reset yourself. When you return your focus will be surer, your vision refreshed and your confidence larger.

YOUR CHALLENGE

Who are you when you are not working? Do you still feel successful? Worthy?

When was the last time you truly relaxed?

Can you think of a time when you stepped away from your work and when you returned, your mind was clearer, your judgement surer?

Schedule time out—and be firm with yourself. Stay away from anything that feeds your addiction!

What can you start doing, stop doing, do more of, and less of? What are all the benefits that will flow?

> *By helping us keep the world in perspective, sleep gives us a chance to refocus on the essence of who we are. And in that place of connection, it is easier for the fears and concerns of the world to drop away.*
>
> ~ Arianna Huffington, businesswoman

LEARN YOUR WAY TO SUCCESS

Learning never exhausts the mind.

~ Leonardo da Vinci

Leonardo was curious about everything. Once he'd understood one thing his mind went in search of new knowledge. Perhaps this is the secret to his longevity. He lived until he was 67, at a time when the life-expectancy was only 39.7 years. And in death he achieved immortality.

Feeling tired? Bored? Fatigued? Try a FTE—first time experience. What have you always wanted to know or learn but never thought you could?

You may surprise yourself and in the process discover a new path to success. Sometimes the best way to reset your life, gain new knowledge, or master a new skill is to gain inspiration from others.

Tim Ferris, an American author, entrepreneur, angel investor, and public speaker, recently shared how creating his podcast, *The Tim Ferris Show*, was his way of taking a break from the stress of his other professional endeavors.

While there was a lot to learn, he was determined to have fun. What started out as a side-gig has now become a phenomenal success. Best of all he says he's always learning new things and being continually inspired.

YOUR CHALLENGE

Stay curious. Put your heart, mind and soul into acquiring new knowledge.

Be patient. Enjoy not knowing. It takes time to acquire mastery.

Anyone can be good, but being awesome takes practice—are you willing to put in 10,000 hours to achieve mastery?

> *Whether you succeed or not is irrelevant, there is no such thing. Making your unknown known is the important thing—and keeping the unknown always beyond you.*
>
> ~ Georgia O'Keeffe, artist

PLAY

I love those who can smile in trouble.

~ Leonardo da Vinci

Did you know that at the age of four, 96 percent of children think they can be anything they want to be, but that by the age of 18 only four percent of them still believe it?

As we grow up and get sensible, we tend to close down our sense of possibility, trading in our dreams and passions for a steady pay check and a "proper job". Somewhere along the way we have lost the ability to play. Playing can seem irresponsible to many people.

But Leonardo da Vinci recognized and embraced the value of play, as did Albert Einstein many years later when he said, "Creativity is intelligence having fun."

Be playful. Cultivate your inner child. Don't take yourself too seriously. Act up a little, goof-off, experiment—if you find yourself in trouble, smile.

Laughter triggers the release of endorphins, the brain's feel good chemicals, setting off an emotional reaction which makes us feel great.

Benefits of play include:

- Boosting your creativity and problem solving skills
- Reducing stress, anxiety, and depression
- Improving your relationships and connections with others
- Bringing more balance, fun, lightness and levity into your life
- Diminishing your worries
- Increasing your ability to do creative and productive work.

LEONARDO WAS A GREAT PRANKSTER, and he loved surrounding himself with other pranksters—people who were young in mind, body and spirit.

This probably explains why he took in a young 10-year-old apprentice who he nicknamed Salai, *The Devil*. He often wrote in his journal how mischievous and naughty, but also how interesting, the young boy was.

Examples of Leonardo's playful creations include the sets for theatrical productions he designed and stages for his wealthy grown-up patrons, including the Duke of Milan and the King of France.

With his playful approach to experimentation and a positive, joyous response to the world around him, Leonardo da Vinci was a dedicated practitioner of his art, working constantly through his life and producing a very large and varied body of work.

As play researcher and psychiatrist Stuart Brown says in his book *Play: How it Shapes the Brain, Opens the Imagination, and Invigorates the Soul*, "A lack of play should be treated like malnutrition: it's a health risk to your body and mind."

CASSANDRA GAISFORD

YOUR CHALLENGE

How can you be more playful—at home and at work?

What benefits will flow?

> *A well-composed book is a magic carpet*
> *on which we are wafted to a world*
> *that we cannot enter in any other way.*
>
> ~ Caroline Gordon, novelist

CHASE THE LIGHT

Darkness steeps everything with its hue, and the more an object is divided from darkness the more it shows its true and natural color.

~ Leonardo da Vinci

What's your default position when things go awry, obstacles challenge your resolve, technology goes belly-up or unforeseen demands on your time derail your plans?

Does your mood darken? Setbacks are normal foes you'll meet on the path to success, but how you greet them will determine the outcome.

Keep your thoughts light. You may need to bring out the big guns to wage war against doubt, despair and other dark, heavy thoughts. While they're often part of the journey to success, you will need to slay them to stay motivated and optimistic.

Leonardo would turn again and again toward the things that created light. He didn't ignore the shadows, but he didn't allow his palette to be overloaded by darkness.

Acceptance, optimism, willpower, grit, stubborn determination and a resolve to persevere are critical skills to cultivate, as is flexibility and the willingness to adapt. Sometimes it's all too hard and you need to hibernate. You can take a lesson from nature in this regard.

YOUR CHALLENGE

Resist complaining and victim talk—it increases toxicity in your mind and body, hampering your progress.

Throw your energy into positivity—strive to engineer and implement solutions, no matter how small.

Ask for help if too much darkness creeps in.

Peer into the darkness and look for the gift

How can you move from darkness towards the light?

Having to fight hard has made me a better architect.

~ Dame Zaha Mohammad Hadid, architect

LEARN FROM FAILURE

I do not depart from my furrow.

~ Leonardo da Vinci

Although Leonardo is widely recognized as one of the world's greatest geniuses, he also made colossal mistakes and suffered staggering failures which would have felled many.

But he persevered anyway. He knew that learning from his own experience also meant learning from his mistakes.

Experimenting with new painting techniques ruined his fresco, *The Battle of Anghiari,* and nearly destroyed *The Last Supper*. His flying machines never got off the ground, and his attempts to divert the Arno River in Florence was a massive public failure.

But he didn't hang up his artist's apron, nor his inventor's cap. He never strayed from his course—he learned from his failures, accepted them as par for the course, hunkered down and continued his quest to learn, experiment and explore.

The furrow he wished to plough was first-hand experience and experimentation—in this path he succeeded.

Reframe failure. The greatest lessons come not from your successes but from your failures. What can you let your failures teach you? Don't look at hurdles as a negative thing but as a reflective tool on how to improve.

Reading biographies of people like Leonardo da Vinci and other people whose success you admire can give you great encouragement along your path to creating your own victories.

YOUR CHALLENGE

Are you prepared to fail in order to succeed?

Do you give yourself permission to learn from mistakes? What is the biggest mistake you ever made and what did you learn?

What new experiences are you prepared to embark on?

What would you do differently if you had no fear of making mistakes?

Whose failure story inspires you? Why? What does it teach you?

I have a lot of things to prove to myself. One is that I can live my life fearlessly.

~ Oprah, businesswoman

PRINCIPLE SIX: EMPOWER YOUR BODY

KEEP YOUR BODY HEALTHY

Good judgement proceeds from clear understanding, and a clear understanding comes from reason derived from sound rules, and sound rules are the daughters of sound experience—the common mother of all the sciences and arts.

~ Leonardo da Vinci

It's tougher to succeed if you lack energy, feel stressed, sluggish, lethargic or unhealthy. Artificially stimulating your mind, body and soul won't cut it in the long term.

Strong agile minds and souls need strong agile bodies to carry them. Leonardo's physical strength, but also his grace and agility was well documented.

Giorgio Vasari, a 16th century historian and architect once wrote, "his great strength could restrain the most violent fury, and he could bend an iron knocker or a horseshoe as if it were lead."

Leonardo's passionate quest to understand human anatomy and extensive knowledge of how the body works made him a "one-stop merchant" in achieving and maintaining ultimate health and well-being.

He was well versed in avoiding extremes—too much sloth made one prone to gluttony, too much activity overwhelmed, and too many vain pleasures taken to extremes were the cause of failure.

YOUR CHALLENGE

What can you stop, start, do more of or less of, to maintain some balance and keep your body healthy?

Do you listen to your body barometer when it tells you to exercise more and sloth around less?

My clients needed to know how to effectively respond to what their intuition was advising, and how they could learn to heal their lives and assist in healing those around them.

~ Dr Mona Lisa Schulz, neuropsychiatrist

STRESS LESS

He who takes medicine is ill advised.

~ Leonardo da Vinci

Leonardo's mind and body appeared never to be at rest. He accomplished more than any man of his time.

But if you read his journals you'll know he was fully aware of the need to stop, take a break, get some rest, eat well, stay away from negative people, keep his mind positive, exercise, do things he loved, play, spend time in nature, experience the quietness of solitude, and many other stress management techniques we are all encouraged to adopt today.

The fact is that stress and success do not make good lovers. Stress-overload has been described as the disease of our modern society. When you are under too much pressure, take too much on and don't take time out, you tend to live your life on overdrive and on the verge of burnout.

When you're stressed you are less effective, make more mistakes, suffer more and are prone to illness.

Very often people turn to 'medicine'—chemical highs, alcohol, and prescription drugs—to manage the symptoms. But the reality is that these only offer temporary relief, masking symptoms which left unresolved can set fire to everything you've worked so hard to achieve.

YOUR CHALLENGE

Would you die for your job? Destroy your relationships? Sacrifice your mental health?

What can you start, stop, do more of, and less of to keep your stress levels at a healthy optimum?

If architecture doesn't kill you, then you're no good.

~ Dame Zaha Mohammad Hadid, architect (died aged 65)

YOU BOOZE YOU LOSE

Here again many vain pleasures are enjoyed, both by the mind in imagining impossible things, and by the body in taking those pleasures that are often the cause of the failing of life. Extremes are to be avoided.

~ Leonardo da Vinci

Alcohol and success don't make good marriage partners, but they're often fatally attracted.

While there's no evidence that Leonardo was a teetotaler, he was a clever man. Experience would have told him what we all know—too much booze muddles the mind, ignites aggression, reduces responsiveness and ultimately depresses.

It's also hard to quit.

Many successful people limit their drinking or consciously decide not to touch a drop. Keeping their resolve takes extraordinary willpower.

US president Donald Trump doesn't drink. Deepak Chopra gave up drinking, saying "I liked it too much."

Julia Cameron, author of *The Artists Way*, fought her way back from alcoholism. Others like Amy Winehouse devastatingly never made it.

Drink to success? Destroying your career, ruining your relationships, sacrificing your sanity, and taking your life is a massive price to pay to celebrate success.

Benefits of not drinking are many, including:

- Authentic happiness
- Increased memory and mental performance
- Better control of your emotions
- Increased productivity
- Sweeter relationships
- Improved confidence, self-esteem
- Stronger ability to focus on your goals and dreams
- Greater intuition and spiritual intelligence

The choice is ultimately yours. Only you know the benefits alcohol delivers or the toll it exacts.

YOUR CHALLENGE

Trial sobriety—take the 30 day challenge. Experiment with living an alcohol-free life

Do you need help to moderate or quit drinking? Consider purchasing any of my books in the Mindful Drinking series, including *Mind Your Drink: The Surprising Joy of Sobriety* and *Mind Over Mojitos: Easy Recipes for Happier Hours & a Joy-Filled Life*

> *I'm proud of people who have the determination and the fearlessness to actually go and face their demons and get better. This is a life or death situation.*
>
> ~ Eva Mendes, actress

MINDFOOD

To keep in health, this rule is wise: eat only when you want and relish food. Chew thoroughly that it may do you good. Have it well cooked, unspiced and undisguised.

~ Leonardo da Vinci

Leonardo knew how magnificent and clever our bodies are. But for everything to fire optimally you need to fuel it with food geared for performance, and not inhale your meal in a race to the finish.

You are what you feed your stomach—which also feeds your mind. Whether you're a vegetarian as Leonardo was, a meat-eater, gluten-free, or something else, ensure you're putting smart fuel into your body.

Modern nutritionists, and health professionals warn of the perils of over and under eating; not eating fresh, seasonal, organic food; and chewing insufficiently.

Diabetes is on the rise. Obesity is an epidemic. Cholesterol and blood pressure is going through the roof. And stress, depression, anxiety and other mental troubles are all trending upward.

Your gut is also your second brain—a major receptor site of dopamine, a neurotransmitter that helps control the brain's reward and pleasure centers. Dopamine also helps regulate feel good feelings we all need to fuel success.

It also regulates movement—enabling you to not only see the rewards of your efforts, but to take action toward them.

Benefits of healthy eating practices include:

- Increased clarity of thinking
- Healthy body weight
- Increased positive emotions
- Enhanced mental, emotional and physical health
- Improved mood
- More energy and stamina
- Improves goal achievement
- Promotes better sleep
- Improves longevity.

YOUR CHALLENGE

Consider booking a check-up with a naturopath or nutritionist. You may be surprised how many allergies are impacting your optimum health.

Remember, your stomach doesn't have teeth—take the time to chew and enjoy your food.

Implement some new healthy eating habits. What can you start, stop, eat more of, less of to fuel your success?

*If you take care of your mind,
you take care of the world.*

~ Arianna Huffington, businesswoman

WATER THERAPY

Water is the driving force in nature.

~ Leonardo da Vinci

Nature was Leonardo's true teacher, and understanding this was key to understanding everything. In particular, he was in awe of the power of water. One of the talents he promoted was his skill as a water engineer.

Later he took his knowledge of hydrodynamics and applied it to the study of blood flow in the heart, noting that lack of blood to the artery which nourishes the heart and surrounding areas caused withering and eventual death.

As blood is to your heart, so water is to your body. Leonardo believed our bodies were machines, designed to run on water and minerals. Because we're made up of 72 percent of water it's vitally important for every important body function.

Insufficient quality water intake, too much coffee or other diuretics, and low consumption of fruit and vegetables can present significant health challenges, robbing your mind and body of energy and vitality.

When you are dehydrated your thoughts can become muddled and you can feel more tired, irritable, demotivated and generally lackluster. Taken to the extreme, lack of water will cause death.

YOUR CHALLENGE

Create more energy and drive by flushing toxins from your body as well as increasing your connection with water. Some simple, but effective strategies include:

- Drinking at least eight glasses of purified water a day
- Reducing alcohol and coffee
- Consuming more fruits and vegetables—as close to raw as possible
- Splash water on your face whenever you're feeling overwhelmed. Cold water steps up circulation, making you feel invigorated
- Swimming in the sea or a lake, bathing in hot mineral water —either a natural spring, or by adding Epsom Salts, a mineral compound of magnesium and sulfate, to your bath.

A well-hydrated, relaxed body and mind will function more effectively.

To understand the things that are at our door is the best preparation for understanding those that lie beyond.

~ Hypatia of Alexandria, astronomer

MOVE INSIDE OUT

This sun gives spirit and life to plants, and the earth nourishes them with moisture.

~ Leonardo da Vinci

How much time do you spend outside, communing with nature? Research has shown that most of us spend 90 percent of our time indoors, and most of it glued to technology.

Leonardo was born in the hills surrounding Florence and spent much of his time walking in the countryside—boosting his spirits, rejuvenating his mind and nourishing his body with outdoor time.

Vitamin D sufficiency, along with diet and exercise has emerged as one of the most important success factors in human health.

Discipline yourself to go out and get some fresh air—ideally somewhere not too frenzied.

Combine brisk walking with deep breathing to boost your energy levels, short-term memory, and state of mind.

When your breathing is calm and steady your body is in a nurtured state, which helps strengthen your immune system.

Researchers also confirm there is a strong link between breathing, outside energy and beneficial brainwave patterns. Which may explain why so many people say that walking is their meditation—clearing their mind, and allowing space for good ideas to flourish.

YOUR CHALLENGE

Monitor how much time you spend indoors.

Schedule regular fresh air time. Improve your breathing, and take a brisk walk to increase levels of oxygen.

> *It was all so far away—there was quiet*
> *and an untouched feel to the country*
> *and I could work as I pleased.*
>
> ~ Georgia O'Keeffe, artist

NOURISH YOURSELF

*If you do not supply nourishment equal to the nourishment that is gone,
life will fail in vigor,
and if you take away this nourishment,
life is entirely destroyed.*

~ Leonardo da Vinci

Sometimes pouring all your energy into your work can consume your inspiration and deplete your mojo. Many people mistakenly turn to the medicine cabinet when their energy reserves are depleted, and their mind, body and soul is malnourished.

Leonardo didn't trust doctors. Given his belief in the power of nature it is likely he turned to natural therapies.

Aromatherapy, using the scents of plants and flowers, is one of many ancient remedies validated by modern science. To replenish his weary mind and stimulate new ideas Leonardo would burn a mixture of juniper and sage, inhaling their sweet, restorative scent.

Nourishment can also be provided by being around people who inspire and encourage you, nourish you goals and put vitality back into your soul.

Topping up and fulfilling your body's spiritual needs is too often neglected. To nourish myself I need to meditate, write in my journal, connect with nature, connect with my SELF. Using essential oils and regular massage with energy workers is another one of many ways I nourish my SELF. Reiki and other energy techniques rebalance energy, realign polarities, and nourish the heart.

YOUR CHALLENGE

What nourishes you?

If you've never tried energy healing do a Leonardo—book a session and let your own experience be your judge.

Investigate the power of smell. Create your own success blend or have an expert create one for you. Beginning with how you want to feel is a good place to start.

Inspirational people are vitamins for the soul. Who can you hang out with? Who do you need to avoid!

What books nourish you?

Holy persons draw to themselves all that is earthly. . . . The earth is at the same time mother.
She is mother of all that is natural, mother of all
that is human. She is the mother of all,
for contained in her are the seeds of all.

~ Hildegard of Bingen, preacher, healer, scientist

SLEEP YOUR WAY TO THE TOP

Time stays long enough for those who use it.

~ Leonardo da Vinci

Many people sacrifice their sleep in the mistaken belief they'll be more productive. But modern science proves conclusively if you skip out on sleep you're compromising not just your efficiency, but also your health.

"We're suffering a sleep crisis," warns Arianna Huffington, the co-founder and editor-in-chief of The Huffington Post, and the author of *The Sleep Revolution: Transforming Your Life One Night at a Time*. The chronic need to be "plugged in" is hurting our health, productivity, relationships and happiness.

A February 2016 study from the Centers for Disease Control and Prevention reported that sleeping less than seven hours a day can lead to an increased risk of obesity, diabetes, high blood pressure, heart disease, stroke and frequent mental distress. None of which will aid your quest for success.

YOUR CHALLENGE

Try a few of Arianna's tips to help ensure you get a great sleep:

- Meditate for 20 minutes in the morning and at the end of the day to defrag and reconnect with yourself
- Get ready for bed 30 minutes before bedtime
- Turn off all devices and leave them outside your bedroom
- Only read physical books in bed instead of using an e-reader
- End the day with gratitude—write down three things you're grateful for
- Have a hot bath with Epsom Salts
- If you wake in the night meditate
- Be ruthless about prioritizing your well-being.

LEONARDO DIDN'T HAVE ELECTRICITY, Facebook, and the gadgets that keep us up at night, but he did know how awesome sleep was. He once asked, "Why does the eye see more clearly when asleep than the imagination when awake?"

Remind yourself of the benefits that will flow while you sleep, and sleep more!

By helping us keep the world in perspective, sleep gives us a chance to refocus on the essence of who we are. And in that place of connection, it is easier for the fears and concerns of the world to drop away.

~ Arianna Huffington, businesswoman

PLANT POWER

I have from an early age abjured the use of meat, and the time will come when men such as I will look upon the murder of animals as they now look upon the murder of men.

~ Leonardo da Vinci

Leonardo was a vegetarian in a culture where killing animals for food and amusement was the norm. "*My body will not be a tomb for other creatures,*" he vowed.

Regardless of Leonardo's motives many people attribute a diet high in vegetables and plant-based proteins and low in meat consumption to their success.

Where once eating meat was associated with strength and power, a growing number of powerful and successful people are embracing the vegetarian or vegan lifestyle.

Former US President Bill Clinton switched to a meat- and dairy-free diet after a health scare. The low-fat, plant-based diet helped him shed weight and restore his damaged heart.

Many famous Olympians and highly successful athletes are also either vegan, vegetarian or cutting meat from their daily diets. Contrary to what many believe it's possible to succeed in the highly intensive and competitive world of sports without meat.

YOUR CHALLENGE

Are you motivated to reconsider how you fuel your body?

I'm not advocating that you must become a vegetarian, but you may want to experiment with a change which may accelerate your success.

Experiment. Instead of animal based proteins check out alternative vegetable and other plant-based food proteins. You may want to keep a food, mood and success journal to monitor the changes and results.

*As long as I live I will have
control over my being.*

~ Artemisia Gentileschi, artist

PRINCIPLE SEVEN: EMPOWER YOUR RELATIONSHIPS

SERVE ONLY ONE MASTER

You cannot serve two masters.

~ Leonardo da Vinci

Some people fear success because they're afraid succeeding might mean having to choose work over intimate relationships. Others fear abandonment.

One of my clients only found her true groove in life when she left an unhealthy marriage—saving her career and her health in the process. Others have found their success is strengthened by the love and support of their significant other.

Only you can determine what your priorities are, how to balance competing demands on your time and energy and what you may, or not may not, have to sacrifice. What matters most is maintaining a healthy self-esteem.

Healthy self-esteem means that you don't have to be in a relationship to feel love. You will always have the love you feel for yourself and (ideally) the love you feel for your work. You'll also attract love to you

—the love and admiration of people who love you for you and for your work.

YOUR CHALLENGE

What beliefs do you have about success and relationships? How can you challenge these beliefs safely?

Who do you admire that works and lives with healthy self-love, regardless of others' value judgements?

Sometimes, women feel they have to do everything—work, manage the house, look after the children—but there's too much to do. So you have to learn early on that you can't do everything yourself, and you have to learn to trust other people to work on your vision.

~ Dame Zaha Mohammad Hadid, architect

FRUITFUL COLLABORATIONS

Minds which in lieu of exercise give themselves up to sloth; for these like the razor lose their keen edge, and the rust of ignorance destroys their form.

~ Leonardo da Vinci

Who do you admire? Who inspires you? What successful people would you like to spend time with—and why?

Leonardo kept counsel with many people he respected and admired: great mathematicians, scientists, poets, architects, alchemists, popes and kings.

One of the most fruitful collaborations of Leonardo's career occurred in 1496 when he met the mathematician Fra Luca Pacioli, during his time in Milan.

Their meeting became a catalyst for a flourishing of Leonardo's interest and development in mathematics. Leonardo was inspired by the combination of Pacioli's empirical approach with a Platonic reverence for the mystery of mathematical order.

Had he not spent time with the great mathematician Leonardo may never have been introduced to this new knowledge, and he wouldn't have been asked to illustrate Pacioli's work, *De Divina Proportione*. Leonardo's drawing of The *Vitruvian Man* is one of his most iconic creations.

The rapid development of Leonardo's anatomical studies was also attributed to his meeting with the exceptionally brilliant young anatomist Marcantonio della Torre.

Your muses don't have to be living, and you don't have to have met them personally. Leonardo was also influenced by Vitruvius, a Roman architect and engineer who died 15 years BC. Vitruvius believed in strength and beauty—ideals that Leonardo also made his own.

Resist the urge to go it alone. Two, three, four and more great minds will always be better than one.

YOUR CHALLENGE

Connect with your heroes. Who can you learn most from? Look at who your muse or hero admires and follow these people too.

Reach out! Read their biography, study their path to success, connect on social-media. Get friendly and cultivate a relationship. Perhaps they'd be willing to mentor you.

Network and collaborate your way to success. Build authentic, powerful relationships with influencers, and turn those relationships into mutually beneficial partnerships.

> *Surround yourself with only people*
> *who are going to lift you higher.*
>
> ~ Oprah, businesswoman

RELATIONSHIP SUCCESS

Realize that everything connects to everything else.

~ Leonardo da Vinci

The health of your relationships is vital to your success. Leonardo da Vinci once said, "Marriage is like putting your hand into a bag of snakes in the hope of pulling out an eel."

Read into this what you will, but the theme is clear. Make good choices and marry well, keep your relationship in good health, or don't marry at all.

Divorce your job, your boss, your partner—anyone who is toxic to your health and happiness. Take the good with the bad, don't give up too easily, work at it and recognize that nothing is absolutely perfect.

But If you can't make things work, be it professionally or personally, be prepared to quit. Feeling like you're always getting your head bitten off, or you're surrounded by a vat of snakes will only impede your success.

YOUR CHALLENGE

How healthy are your relationships?

Who is positively affecting your life?

Who, or what, do you need to divorce?

> *Women are always told, 'You're not going to make it, it's too difficult, you can't do that, don't enter this competition, you'll never win it.' They need confidence in themselves and people around them to help them to get on.*
>
> ~ Dame Zaha Mohammad Hadid, architect

CONFLICT HAPPENS

*Nothing can be loved or hated
unless it is first understood.*

~ Leonardo da Vinci

While you need others to survive and thrive, success in work and in life is more likely when your relationships are harmonious. As much as we all like to get on, sometimes conflict is inevitable.

People may feel threatened by your success, they may deliberately try to thwart you, or they may misunderstand your motives and desires.

Your family and loved ones may resent the time you need to spend away from them. You may feel guilty for wanting more from your life.

As Leonardo said, the noblest pleasure is the joy of understanding. Seek first to understand, and then plan your conflict-handling strategy.

YOUR CHALLENGE

What do others fear? How might this fear or anxiety bring 0ut the worst in them?

How might they want the best for you?

What are their agendas? How might they want the worst for you? Why might your success threaten them?

How sharp are your conflict resolution skills?

How are you unnecessarily or unknowingly creating conflict?

Learn from your experiences.

Perhaps others need to see, touch, feel, taste and smell your success before they can back you. Perhaps you do too! Succeed anyway!

I am a woman in process. I'm just trying like everybody else. I try to take every conflict, every experience, and learn from it. Life is never dull.

~ Oprah Winfrey, businesswoman

THE LITMUS TEST

Falsehood puts on a mask.
Nothing is hidden under the sun.

~ Leonardo da Vinci

It's not easy to sever ties with people who were once close to you. But sometimes the 'friendliest people' can be saboteurs. Use the litmus test —analyze the overall quality of your friendships.

Are your friends, family, and other people close to you positive or acidic and toxic. Do they elevate your self-belief and confidence or are they a dead weight?

Do they cheerlead your successes? Encourage you when you stumble? Are they genuinely pleased to see you trying to achieve the dreams, desires or ambitions you hold dear? Or do they warn you of the perils of trying to fly?

Leonardo distanced himself from many people, including his family. He was always the black sheep—the illegitimate bastard. Even his father left him out of his will, and later when Leonardo's uncle made him sole heir of his estate, Leonardo's siblings fought for their share.

Instead of bemoaning his fate, or trying relentlessly to please them, he severed ties with those most toxic to him. I've had to do the same, as have many successful people.

Your time and energy is often better spent succeeding than striving to sweeten relationships that have turned sour.

Take comfort in the fact that often it's about them, not you. Resolve to speak no evil—if they are vile toward you, thank them for the lessons they are teaching you, wish them well and get on with your beautiful life.

I can't give you the formula for success, but I can failure. Try to please everyone you meet.

YOUR CHALLENGE

What impact do toxic people have in your life? Do they erode your confidence? Self-esteem? Foster great self-doubt?

Who do you need to cut ties with? It doesn't always need to be physically. Although many successful people have had to move away from their family of origin to fly. Consider what and how you need to sever your connection from—emotionally, energetically, or spiritually.

Accept failure as part and parcel of life. It's not the opposite of success; it's an integral part of success.

~ Arianna Huffington, businesswoman

VALIDATE YOURSELF

He who truly knows has no occasion to shout.

~ Leonardo da Vinci

Validate and empower your relationship with yourself. When you have healthy self-esteem you have mastered the art of self-love.

You don't need to shout your worth from the roof-tops. You don't need to say, 'Look at me! Look at me!' And you don't need the validation of others to succeed.

"Many people want to please their peers, they want to please other successful people, they want to be recognized by academia or hear everyone tell them how good they are. Forget about it. Who cares? You are here to share your soul—not to please others," encourages the author of *The Alchemist*, Paulo Coehlo.

Your willingness to grow, change, take risks, and be open to all aspects of your soul, regardless of the opinions of others, is a sign of healthy self-esteem and your belief in your vision.

Criticism won't stop you in your tracks, praise won't sway you from your mission, your authentic work created with love and self-belief will magnetize customers and loyal fans to you. Infuse everything you do with your beautiful energy.

YOUR CHALLENGE

How can you be your biggest fan?

What three things can you do today to validate yourself?

What three things do you need to let go of in order to care less about what others think?

Understand that the right to choose your own path is a sacred privilege. Use it. Dwell in possibility.

~ Oprah Winfrey, businesswoman

SOCIAL SAVVY

*Words that do not satisfy the ear of the hearer
weary him or vex him.*

~ Leonardo da Vinci

Leonardo was unique, different and unusual. He stood out from the crowd simply by following his curiosity and daring to challenge the norm. In doing so he attracted fans as well as rivals.

If you are original, different, or unusual in some way, your tendency to stand out from the crowd can make you a more visible target.

You may attract people who are jealous of you, and may act out angrily or violently to try and sabotage your success.

Staying strong and grounded while still keeping true to your unique vision and quest requires resilience, and the ability to develop 'social savvy.'

This is where cultivating the right mindset is important. If you think like a victim, or believe that you get scapegoated in family or other social groups you will find it difficult to get along with others and live in society.

An important diplomatic skill to master, says psychiatrist and neuroscientist Dr Mona Lisa Schulz, is assertiveness—the ability to say the right thing to the right person with the right amount of emotional intensity.

YOUR CHALLENGE

How assertive are you? Do you know how to handle another person's anger, jealousy or hostility? Socially savvy people who are diplomatic either address it directly, diffuse it (humor, compassion etc.) or ignore it.

Their strategy differs depending on the situation. Whatever strategy you choose ensure that you don't become so paralyzed by conflict that you become submissive, defensive, or in any way disempowered.

Critically—do not give up, or fade into obscurity. To survive in any society, or in your family tribe, master the art of knowing when to blend in, and when to be courageously different

How can you still feel good about yourself if someone is angry with you, discouraging, or jealous of your success?

A combination of good timing, flexibility, and empathy makes some people socially brilliant.

~ Dr. Mona Lisa Schulz, neuroscientist

BELONG TO YOURSELF

If you are alone you belong entirely to yourself. If you are accompanied by even one companion you belong only half to yourself or even less in proportion to the thoughtlessness of his conduct.

~ Leonardo da Vinci

You may have heard people say that you're only as successful as the five people you associate with.

As you've read, Leonardo kept counsel with many people he respected and admired. Spending time with these people no doubt fueled his interest, inspired desire, and propelled his success.

But when it came time to do his work, he did it alone, and he did it his way. To succeed you must know when, and how, to spend time with others and when to immerse yourself in solitude.

When you do spend time with others, chose carefully. Don't dilute your energy. Too much group think can stifle your confidence, motivation and originality.

Being solitary is not the same as being a loner. Learn from others but cultivate a good relationship with yourself.

YOUR CHALLENGE

Set aside some regular "you" time.

Keep your own counsel.

Love you more.

Love wins. It does win.
We know it wins.

~ J.K. Rowling, author

BALANCING RESPONSIBILITES TO OTHERS

In serving others I cannot do enough.

~ Leonardo da Vinci

Leonardo was devoid of family responsibilities—he never married and he had no children. Although he did feel responsible for housing, feeding and paying the salaries of his assistants.

If you're like me, and have family—sons or daughters at home, aging parents, in-laws, or a spouse and partner—you'll know how hard it is to balance everybody's needs. So many people, women in particular, feel guilty putting their needs first.

But somewhere you have to take time for you! If you aways give, give to others, there'll come point when the well is dry. At some point you have to prioritize your needs, dreams and ambitions—and your sanity. Leonardo knew this too. No matter how much you have on your dinner plate you can make room for you.

YOUR CHALLENGE

Are mistaken beliefs about pursuing your own desires holding you back?

Are you being a martyr? Doing everything for everyone? Or do you delegate and enlist others to help?

> *The moment you are old enough to take the wheel, responsibility lies with you.*
>
> ~ J.K. Rowling, author

STAY AHEAD OF THE COMPETITION

What is fair in men, passes away, but not so in art.

~ Leonardo da Vinci

You must know what others are doing in order to perform better. Learn from your competitors.

Work-wise you are in competition for the discretionary income of current and future customers, just as Leonardo was. He constantly innovated to stay ahead of his rivals. But he drew ideas from them too.

Relationship-wise you may be in competition with people who want what you've got.

Knowing your competition should not be something that stresses you out. Understanding what others are doing right, or different from you can inspire.

You'll know when to lift your game and when to shape-shift and start anew. When too many like-minded talents flood the market, you may 'do a Leonardo'—diversify, adapt and move.

Michelangelo, Raphael, Botticelli and other artists all competed with

Leonardo for sought after commissions that only a few wealthy patrons could provide.

During his later years in Milan, Leonardo fell out of favor with the Medici pope. But once again he turned his misfortunate into fortune, aligning with the French king and moving to France where his competitors would be few. There he created some of his best art and began at last to compile his lifetime's work into his treatise.

YOUR CHALLENGE

Here's a few ways to stay ahead of the competition:

- Keep your eyes on your rivals
- Know your stakeholders and treat them well
- Differentiate yourself from your competitors
- Step up your marketing
- Target new markets
- Diversify and expand your offer
- Look to the future
- Innovate—be a pioneer
- Keeping improving—good art endures.

Life is an unfoldment, and the further we travel the more truth we can comprehend. To understand the things that are at our door is the best preparation for understanding those that lie beyond.

~ Hypatia of Alexandria, astronomer

PRINCIPLE SEVEN: EMPOWER YOUR WORK

BE ORIGINAL

The painter will produce pictures of little merit if he takes the works of others as his standard.

~ Leonardo da Vinci

Originality and authenticity was a crucial part of Leonardo's success. HIs obsessive search for original truth, understanding and invention led him to create things other thought were crazy or impossible—but later copied or followed.

A big part of authenticity is following your own truth. If you think something is a great idea—try it. Don't get bogged down subscribing to other people's ideas and taking their work as your standard.

Be a trailblazer like all the great inventors, and have the satisfaction of being authentically you.

History is richer because of people, like Leonardo da Vinci, who strode forward despite others rejecting their attempts, laughing at their vision, or criticizing them personally and professionally. Original thinkers, feelers and believers always see things others don't.

YOUR CHALLENGE

Determine who you are and who you choose to be.

Create a life or work of heart that is as original as you are. Believe in your capacity for originality.

Take your opinion as your standard. Bring forth your passion and infuse your life and work with true essence—all else will follow.

I had no idea that being your authentic self could make me as rich as I've become. If I had, I'd have done it a lot earlier.

~ Oprah Winfrey, businesswoman

LIST YOUR THINGS TO DO

It is useful to constantly observe, note, and consider.

~ Leonardo da Vinci

Leonardo used to travel with a small notebook hanging from his belt so that whenever something caught his eye he could make a note, or record it visually. His genius lay in knowing that not everything that could be recorded and stored in the mind.

His mind was restlessly hungry. There were so many things he wanted to do. So that no opportunity was left untapped his notebooks and journals served as his 'to do' list.

Here's a few things translated from the tumble of thoughts recorded in his journals:

- Draw Milan
- Find a master of hydraulics and get him to tell you how to repair a lock, canal and mill
- Ask about the measurement of the sun

Leonardo, like other great brains, allowed his mind to free-range. No single idea could hold his interest indefinitely. The task and challenge of marshaling his thoughts into a coherent, structured whole fell to others.

Forcing yourself to concentrate prematurely can inhibit your imagination. Far better, Leonardo and other creativity experts maintain, to record inspiration as it strikes, in a to-do-sometime-in the-future list.

Studies, including one by Dr. Holly White, then at the University of Memphis, found that minds that break-free, that naturally wander, can often achieve more than those which are more ordered, structured—and arguably, inhibited.

YOUR CHALLENGE

Where do you record your great ideas? Small seeds of inspiration can blossom into formidable majesty.

Sustain you focus and future potential by jotting thoughts down, as and when they occur, for future reference.

*I found I could say things with color
and shapes that I couldn't say any other way—things I had no words for.*

~ Georgia O'Keeffe, artist

MAKE YOUR JOB WORK FOR YOU

As you cannot do what you want,
Want what you can do.

~ Leonardo da Vinci

Leonardo cultivated successful relationships and actively sought wealthy benefactors to finance his ambitions. He worked for tyrants, murderers and fools when he needed to finance his passions.

While he loved his freedom he was also a pragmatist. Court appointments were in many ways an ideal position for Leonardo. They took away the pressure of depending upon erratic commissions which independent artists relied on.

By taking away money worries, and coming under the protection of powerful rulers, it gave him time to explore all of his passions and interests while earning a steady salary.

On the flip-side though, much of this time was consumed fulfilling his employers' desires. Sometimes these bosses, like Cesare Borgia, were tyrannical murderers— conflicting with Leonardo's values.

Leonardo knew that maintaining a positive attitude was critical, as was making sure his passion projects weren't neglected.

"Evil thinking is either envy or ingratitude", he once wrote. He was grateful for those who paid his bills, but the pursuit of gold was never his primary driver.

If you can't have what you want, learn to love what you've got. Attitude is queen.

YOUR CHALLENGE

If you feel trapped or stifled by your current job or boss, how can you maintain a positive mindset?

How can you finance your passions?

Do you need to make peace with those who pay your bills?

Don't be afraid to take time to learn. It's good to work for other people. I worked for others for 20 years. They paid me to learn.

~ Vera Wang, designer

THE MONEY OR YOUR LIFE

It may be that I shall possess less than other men of more peaceful lives, or than those who want to grow rich in a day. I may live for a long time in great poverty, as always happens, and to all eternity will happen, to alchemists, the would-be creators of gold and silver.

~ Leonardo da Vinci

Money gives you choices, but the pursuit of wealth is not everything. Like Leonardo, having mountains of gold and silver may not be your primary motivator.

Throughout this book I've encouraged you to work out what is really true for you. Prioritizing the value you place on money, amassing a fortune and material wealth may create a massive mindset shift.

YOUR CHALLENGE

What are the hidden costs of always striving for money?

What can you start, stop, do more, less of to earn less but live more?

. . .

IF LACK of finances are a challenge for you you'll find plenty of creative and practical ways to do more with less, or generate more cash-flow in my *Mid-Life Career Rescue* trilogy —getBook.at/CareerRescueBox.

You only have what you give.
It's by spending yourself that you become rich.

~ Isabel Allende, author

STEAL LIKE AN ARTIST

He is a poor pupil who does not go beyond his master.

~ Leonardo da Vinci

A foundation step to fast-track success is to follow the things you love and learn from those who have made this love a key part of their success.

"School is one thing. Education is another", writes Austin Kleon in, *Steal Like an Artist*. Acquire knowledge as Leonardo did. Learn your way to success.

Leonardo started his career as a child copying and drawing nature. His inspiration drove his quest. He followed his curiosity and the things he loved.

Early in his career he was apprenticed to Andrea del Verrocchio, from whom Leonardo copied how to make brushes, prepare paint, draw, sculpt and paint.

The story of Leonardo surpassing his master is legendary—the angel he added to Verrocchio's painting (*Baptism of Christ*, c. 1473) was so much better that the master never painted again.

At the young age of 21 Leonardo designed and completed a painting on his own, T*he Annunciation*. Just think how much slower his progress would have been had he not studied under a master.

You may not have access to a mentor or teacher physically, but you can align mentally, emotionally, and spiritually.

YOUR CHALLENGE

Read biographies, study the work of those whose success you'd love to emulate. Think about your favorite heros and heroines—in business and in life. Google everything!

Copycat your way to success and then take it a step further. What did they miss? What could have been better? What didn't they do? If all your favorite muses got together what would they be making today?

Then go make that stuff.

I do not try to dance better than anyone else. I only try to dance better than myself.

~ Arianna Huffington, businesswoman

STEP BY STEP

If you wish to go to the top of a building, you must go up step by step; otherwise it will be impossible that you should reach the top.

~ Leonardo da Vinci

So many people rush in the climb for success, ignoring planning and tripping over their lack of knowledge, and the practical skills that must be learned. Anyone can be good but being exceptional takes diligence.

Leonardo da Vinci said that if you wish to pursue your craft, and have a sound knowledge of a subject, you need to identify the details you need to master.

Begin at the first step, "And do not go onto the second step till you have the first well fixed in memory and in practice. And if you do otherwise you will throw away your time, or certainly greatly prolong your studies. And remember to acquire diligence rather than rapidity."

Avoid being controlled and dictated to by the relentless ticking clock. Little steps are more effective than grand leaps so don't become disheartened or be deterred if your progress is slower than others. Do something every day, no matter how small, to keep your dreams alive.

YOUR CHALLENGE

What does being diligent mean to you?

Have you identified all the knowledge and skills and steps you need to master in order to achieve your successful outcome?

Are you patient or impatient? How could rushing to the outcome trip you up?

Today we often use deadlines—real and imaginary—to imprison ourselves.

~ Arianna Huffington, businesswoman

DO WHAT YOU ARE

The acquisition of knowledge is always of use to the intellect, because it may thus drive out useless things and retain the good.

~ Leonardo da Vinci

While Leonardo clearly didn't have access to modern personality tests, he was a master in the realms of observation. He knew what gave him energy, how he preferred to take in information, make decisions and organize his life.

The Myers-Briggs Type Indicator is one of the most popular preference-based tools. Experts differ in whether Leonardo's personality preferences were INTP (Introverted, Intuitive, Thinking, and Perceiving), or ISTP (Introverted, Sensing, Thinking, and Perceiving), or even an ENTP (Extroverted, Intuitive, Thinking, and Perceiving.

I know some of these terms may be foreign to you. See the Further Resources section at the end of this book for more information about The Myers-Briggs Type Indicator, or turn to Google.

While guessing people preferences accurately is not possible, my bet is Leonardo's leaned toward INTP. His thinking was highly introverted and intuitive as evidenced by his prolific recording of thoughts and ideas recorded in his extensive collection of journals.

His thoughts were diverted into many areas of interest and many of his works remain uncompleted—something that would drive a Judging type crazy. And he preferred the company of special friends and colleagues rather than the mass gatherings and membership of large groups.

Also he was an outlier in so many areas.

Research suggests that less than 10 percent of the population are (INTPs) Introverted, Intuitive, Thinking, and Perceivers—putting Leonardo once again at odds with mainstream folk. More so in Italy, which as a country shares a reported dominant preference for ENFP.

Neuropsychologist, Katherine Benziger says, "People are happiest, healthiest and most effective when developing, using and being rewarded for using their natural gifts." This is very true.

The more you know about yourself the happier you'll be. The better your decisions will be and the more chance you will have of presenting yourself and your natural talents in the best light to people—including yourself.

YOUR CHALLENGE

What are your natural gifts? What are your super powers?

How can you do and be what you are?

See the Further Resources section at the end of this book for more information about The Myers Briggs Type Indicator.

Find something that you love to do, and find a place that you really like to do it in. Your work has to be compelling. You spend a lot of time doing it.

~ Ursula Burns, CEO

KNOW WHEN TO QUIT

Art is never finished, only abandoned.

~ Leonardo da Vinci

Leonardo was criticized for the number of times he left work unfinished. But given his personality preferences and motivations, the chances are high he got bored.

Leonardo thrived on solving challenging problems, starting and visualizing new work, more than he did in the operational tasks required for completion.

He also liked to be his own master, and create work in line with his far-reaching and unconventional vision.

Back in the 15th century the role of an artist during the Renaissance was only just beginning to change from mere tool-boy, to master artisan and rockstar.

Many of Leonardo's patrons had control over the subject matter of what he painted, and how he was to paint it—including the minerals and colors.

These, and the many other constraints exerted upon a creative thinker, free-spirit and highly intelligent man like Leonardo, killed his joy.

Records show he was not always paid for his work, and often struggled financially. Whatever the reasons for his disinterest in continuing with projects, Leonardo knew when to quit.

He was also a strategic player, seldom did he move on without something else to go to. Abandoning displeasing, late-paying clients for more lucrative practical realities was a smart move. As was diversifying and setting the bar higher.

Refusing to settle for mediocrity sustained him—as it will you.

YOUR CHALLENGE

If you're bored, if you don't feel a shiver of excitement or fear, if there's no emotional risk involved, let it go…abandon ship.

If you're struggling to pay the bills, know when to persevere or when it's best to quit You can always return, as Leonardo did, when the timing is better.

> *You are the storyteller of your own life, and you can create your own legend, or not.*
>
> ~ Isabel Allende, author

GET OUT OF YOUR OWN WAY

*Fortune is powerless to help one
who does not exert himself.*

~ Leonardo da Vinci

So many people who took The Art of Success Questionnaire asked me, "How do I get out of my own way?" Inspiration has to find you working. It won't come any faster or slower with excuses, tricks, 'pretend' deadlines, or bribes.

As Paulo Coelho, author of *The Alchemist*, said on *The Tim Ferris Show* recently, "I have the book inside me, I start procrastinating in the morning. I check my emails, I check news—I check anything that I could check just to avoid the moment to sit and face myself as a writer in front of my book.

For three hours I am trying to tell myself, 'No, no, no. Later. Later. Later.' Then later not to lose face in front of myself I tell myself to sit and write for half an hour, and of course this half an hour becomes 10 hours in a row. That's why I write my books so quickly. Very quickly, because I cannot stop. I cannot stop."

YOUR CHALLENGE

Hack through your excuses: "You're too tired. You don't have time. You're not feeling inspired. It's not good enough. It's not perfect." Or whatever stories you tell yourself to avoid working.

Your excuses are your saboteurs. Your doubts—your traitors. Just do the work. But do it well and do it to the best of your abilities. It's amazing how much can be achieved when you stop resisting.

Identify how you get in your own way. Be honest.

Make a commitment to overcome your SELF.

Make a commitment to really follow your dream.

Do the work! Set a time-limit if it helps. Just 30 minutes—then watch as you get carried away.

The days you work are the best days.

~ Georgia O'Keeffe, artist

PATIENT PERSERVERANCE

Patience preserves us against insults precisely as clothes do against the cold. For if you multiply your garment as the cold increases, that cold cannot hurt you; in the same way increase your patience under great offences, and they cannot hurt your feelings.

~ Leonardo da Vinci

Knowing when to quit is one thing; knowing when to persevere another. Whether it's the weight of obstacles you face, the setbacks and the disappointments, the successes others seem to more speedily achieve, or the critical feedback from others impatient to see more evidence you'll make it—never give up.

Never, never, never give up.

Many of Leonardo's greatest and most enduring successes took years and years to achieve. For over four years he persevered with painting The Mona Lisa. And while modern critics claim he never finished it, it doesn't seem to have mattered in the end.

It wasn't good enough. It was better.

Through his patience, persistence and perseverance he, and his artworks, have achieved immortality.

YOUR CHALLENGE

Keep your mind on your vision, your body moving towards your dreams, your heart warmed by the joy you will feel when you finally achieve success. Most of all enjoy whatever you choose to be, have or do.

Every day see and feel your dream as though it is already achieved, hear the feedback you will receive, taste the victory of your success.

This will keep your faith alive, empower your dreams with your energy, fortify your tenacity—attracting what and who you need, when you need it.

If self-doubt increases, confidence wanes or some other saboteur infects your psyche, dig into your toolkit and multiply your armor. Fortify yourself. Increase your patience—persist and persevere. Success could be just around the corner.

When you think of patience, perseverance and success who comes to mind?

Who or what can help you to manifest more persistence?

Identify three ways to strengthen your persistence by strengthening your willpower and self-discipline.

He who wishes to be rich within a day,
will be hanged within a year.

~ Leonardo da Vinci, inventor

PURSUE YOUR TRUTH

*Fire destroys all sophistry, that is, deceit;
and maintains truth alone, that is gold.
Truth at last cannot be hidden.*

~ Leonardo da Vinci

Truth is where the magic is. "Truth—the sun. Falsehood—a mask", Leonardo once wrote in his journal. Take off your mask, forget about pleasing others. Please yourself.

The pursuit of truth is not always comfortable as many of the great trail-blazers can testify.

All the successful men and women I admire, Leonardo da Vinci included, have searched for and followed their truth—and fought for it. They would rather be failures at something they believed in, then amass success built on a brittle pyre of lies.

Success doesn't come in a manual with fail-safe instructions and money-back guarantees. But there is one truth no one can deny—when you work with integrity and imbue your efforts with love you draw others to you.

As I've already mentioned, love is the highest, most powerful vibration on earth. When you work with love people feel it. It infuses everything you do and attracts people who are magnetized by this potent energy to you.

That's why love, truth and beauty are the best marketing tools around.

Here's a few things following your truth may do for you:

- Liberate you
- Liberate others
- Empower your success
- Lead you to discover new realities
- Energize you
- Attract like-minded people to you
- Boost your courage, confidence and self-belief
- Fill your soul with fire and your heart with passion.

YOUR CHALLENGE

If you wish to succeed in business and life there are two questions you must ask: who are you and are you following your truth?

Choose to fulfill your potential and make something of your life. I believe in you. Go create joy, beauty, love, and magic!

> *The best way to change it is to do it. Right? And then after a while you become it, and it's easy.*
>
> ~ Ursula Burns, CEO

COLOR YOUR SUCCESS

*Among the various studies of natural processes,
that of light gives most pleasure to those who contemplate it.*

~ Leonardo da Vinci

The magical power of color to transform, uplift and empower is something Leonardo was intimately acquainted with.

Psychologists, marketers and brand gurus all know that surrounding yourself with the right colors can mean the difference between failure and success.

Research reveals that it only takes 90 seconds to assess and make a subconscious visual judgement, and a massive 62 to 90 percent of that judgement is based on color alone.

People's beliefs about the power of color to boost their success include:

- 92 percent believe color presents an image of impressive quality
- 90 percent feel color can assist in attracting new customers

- 90 percent believe customers remember presentations and documents better when color is used
- 83 percent believe color makes them appear more successful
- 81 percent think color gives them a competitive edge
- 76 percent believe that the use of color makes their business appear larger to clients

And let's not forget how surrounding yourself with color makes you feel. Add to this the potent power of naturally occurring minerals, gems and metamorphic rocks mined from the earth, and you have potent alchemy.

Mona Lisa continues to be one of the world's most memorable and enchanting portraits. It's no coincidence that Leonardo painted the mesmerising bright blue sky surrounding her with Lapis lazuli. Sadly, time has diluted the original color but the magic remains.

Lapis Lazuli (a bright blue metamorphic rock consisting largely of lazurite) is known as the 'visionary's stone.' It is associated with wisdom and spiritual insight, the promotion of truth, and is also believed to strengthen the mind, enhance psychic abilities, and enable a higher connection with your Higher Self and Spirit Guides.

These are principles and abilities that Leonardo valued highly. It's no coincidence that he painted the powerful blue sky surrounding the Mona Lisa with Lapis lazuli. Mona Lisa continues to be one of world's most enchanting portraits.

Colors have such an impact on your emotions and actions that it makes sense to wear your success colors. Leonardo loved purples—colours associated with nobility as well as the ability to access higher levels of spirituality.

Me? I love gold. Gold makes me feel enriched, nourished, blessed, strong. I used to live in a gold house, and when I need a boost of morale I put on my gold dress! Whatever works, right?!

YOUR CHALLENGE

What is your success color?

How could you surround yourself with more of this color to fuel your success?

> *The best color in the whole world,*
> *is the one that looks good, on you!*
>
> ~ Coco Chanel, fashion designer

YOUR BEAUTY SPOT

What induces you, oh man, to depart from your home in town, to leave parents and friends, and go to the countryside over mountains and valleys, if it is not for the beauty of the world of nature.

~ Leonardo da Vinci

YOUR BEAUTY SPOT IS YOUR POINT OF BRILLIANCE

If you've read my other books you'll know that I've always loved what the artist and philosopher John Ruskin once said, "Where talent, interest and motivation intersect expect a masterpiece."

Using this as your guide, you may like to draw three circles. List your areas of motivation in one (passion, purpose, values, goals etc.); Your interests and obsessions in another; Your favorite skills and talents in the third.

Note where they overlap. This is your internal world, and what I have in the past called your PassionPoint, or Point of Brilliance.

It's also your beauty spot. It's where love lives. It's the union of your soul—your path with heart which leads you toward your higher purpose. As Leonardo said, without love, what then? It's where your light shines brightest.

Surround these three circles with a fourth to enclose them. This symbolizes the external world—both the practical earth and the higher heavens. So many people have speculated on and sensationalized Leonardo's greatest works, looking for clues to interpret and break codes to discover sacred mysteries.

But as Leonardo said himself, the truth is best left in the open. That which is above is the same as that which is below. And this is where beauty and success unite.

Leonardo remains an enigma. But we do know he communed with the Universe, saw into the future, and worked damned hard to master his talents and bring his visions into living realities.

HOW CAN YOUR POINT OF BRILLIANCE SERVE?

To generate career options, knowing what will be needed or in demand, now and in the future, can yield gold.

What needs can you fulfill when you're aligned with your beauty spot? What economic, demographic, social, environmental or other needs can you serve? This is the work you are called to do and where you will truly shine.

It doesn't need to have a massive job title, or be about saving the world. But whatever you choose to do has to fulfill a need. Economics 101—no need, no demand.

Of course, if money is no barrier, you are freer to pursue your own needs without this added focus. By doing this you may just create a demand, or make the world a happier place. Importantly, you'll be happy.

Remember Your Criteria for Success

So many people embark on one path only to find it cuts or suffocates other choices. Others mistakenly believe that you can't have a multitude of passions.

Be clear about who you are, what success means to you, your criteria for fulfillment and begin with this end in mind. Work backwards from the future to implement your success strategy.

CONCLUSION

CONCLUSION: BEAUTY AND THE BEST

"The heavens often rained down the richest gifts on human beings, naturally, but sometimes with lavish abundance bestow upon a single individual beauty, grace and ability, so that, whatever he does, every action is so divine that he distances all other men, and clearly displays how his genius is the gift of God and not a requirement of human art."

~ Giorgio Vasari, *Lives of The Artists*

The belief in the creative, regenerative and divine (transcendental) power of beauty was central to everything Leonardo da Vinci pursued.

Inspired by Vitruvius and the architecture of success grounded in the ancient wisdom of Pythagorean and Platonic mathematical principals, Leonardo knew that nature held the immortal secrets of both beauty and power.

While Leonardo is arguably most famous as an artist, he was the archetype of a Renaissance man, whose unquenchable curiosity was equalled only by the power of his imagination and aptitude for invention.

He gave birth to knowledge that some 500 years later is enjoying its own renaissance, and is validated by modern science (itself only a relatively young 300 years old).

Beauty is timeless, holding sacred universal wisdom and truth. The artist Paul Klee once said, 'One eye sees and the other feels'. And it is this ability to make us care where Leonardo has surpassed many others.

BEAUTY AND YOUR SUCCESS

Beauty comes from the inside. It's your essence—so authentic that, just as there will never be another Leonardo, there will never be another you.

The art of success lies in bringing more beauty into this world. It lies in being you. It's a secret that ancient masters and philosophers understood well. And it's a secret that modern day successful people also know and harness.

Businessmen and women, politicians, and the most successful artists understand that intrinsic, authentic, soulful beauty attracts. Beauty is irresistible. Beauty sells.

You may not be aiming to create the next *Mona Lisa*, but if you infuse your life and your work with your energy, power, talent and essence, who knows—500 years from today somebody may well be writing a book about you and the legacy you left.

You may think the outcome has to happen in a certain way, on a certain day, to reach your goal. But human willpower cannot make everything happen. Spirit has its own idea, of how the arrow flies, and upon what wind it travels.

It may not happen overnight, but if you maintain your focus, and take inspired action, and follow your heart, your time will come.

I promise!

If due to some strange twist of fate, it doesn't? At least you'll know you tried.

CASSANDRA GAISFORD

A life of no regrets—now that's worth striving for.

Let the beauty you love be the life that you live. Now go out and create great art!

IN GRATITUDE AND WITH LOVE,

Cassandra

THE TRUTH ABOUT SUCCESS

The love of virtue. It never looks at any vile or base thing, but rather clings always to pure and virtuous things and takes up its abode in a noble heart; as the birds do in green woods on flowery branches. And this Love shows itself more in adversity than in prosperity; as light does, which shines most where the place is darkest.

~ Leonardo da Vinci

I've distilled Leonardo's principles for success down to twenty-one facts…or TRUTHS as I call them. And the wonderful thing is that these truths can be embodied by you. You can be, have and do whatever your heart desires if you're determined to succeed and look for ways to put these truths into practice.

1 Love

2 Talent

#3 Curiosity

#4 Learning

#5 Interest

#6 Vision

7 Service/Purpose

8 Opportunity

#9 Focus

#10 Commitment

#11 Values

#12 Motivation

#13 Labour

#14 Asking

#15 Goals

#16 Optimism

#17 Virtue/Integrity

#I18 Instinct

#19 Gratitude

#20 Energy

#21 Play

I KNOW you can succeed at whatever you set your heart, mind and soul to. Pursue your liberty—be free to be you. Have the courage and confidence to define success on your own terms.

Follow your passions, cultivate your natural and dormant talents, remain curious and embrace learning, follow your interests, maintain your vision, work with purpose and be of service.

When opportunity knocks, open the door. If it doesn't knock, go out and create opportunities. Focus on what you desire, not what you fear. Commit—devote yourself to your quest for success.

Let your values guide you—they are your truth-compass. Clarify what motivates you, be this extrinsic or intrinsic rewards. Do the work—no matter how small the effort, in time you will amass success.

Ask your way to success, and learn from those with the skill, knowledge and power to help you. Don't be shy, proud or nervous to ask for help!

Set goals—little, bigger and bigger still. Stretch and grow and strive to make the impossible possible. Celebrate your successes along the way —no matter how small.

Cultivate optimism—water it regular and never let faith and hope wither from neglect.

Maintain your integrity and virtue. Follow your hunches, intuition and instinct. Be grateful for all that you have—be it health, friends, support, or your cat.

Maximize your energy—look after your mind, body and soul. And lastly, but perhaps also firstly, play.

Alleviate the pressure—don't take yourself too seriously. Be joyful in success—and also while attempting success. Keep your feet on the ground, your head in the clouds and ride the magic carpet of your creative imagination.

But most of all, 'do a Leonardo'—stand out from the crowd and dare to be different!

*Secretly we're all a little more absurd
then we make ourselves out to be.*

~ J.K. Rowling, author

If the painter wishes to see beauties that charm him, it lies in his power to create them, and if he wishes to see monstrosities that are frightful, ridiculous, or truly pitiable, he is lord and God thereof.

~ Leonardo da Vinci, 1472

II

BOOK TWO: COCO CHANEL

AUTHOR'S NOTE

Those on whom legends are built are their legends.

~ Coco Chanel, businesswoman

Gabrielle Bonheur "Coco" Chanel. Coco had to overcome obstacles to success just like you and I. She suffered many hardships, including the death of her mother when she was young, being abandoned by a father who didn't love her, growing up in an orphanage, and the stigma of her early years which plagued her throughout her life.

She suffered extreme poverty, self-doubt, low-self esteem and craved love. People jealous of her talent also spread malicious rumors and tried to undermine her success.

But she didn't let obstacles stop her from doing the work she loved. The pursuit of excellence born from her experience, fueled by her determination to be an independent woman, and the desire to liberate others, ultimately led to her success.

Her boundless imagination, strength of purpose and courageous spirit are an inspiration to young and old.

Coco Chanel can help people like you and I succeed—personally and professionally.

Successful artists have always struggled, but they persevered anyway. And it is this willingness to pursue their calling in the face of many challenges that holds lessons for us all.

HOW THIS BOOK WILL HELP YOU

Whenever I'm in a slump or needing an inspirational boost I turn to people who are smarter or more skilled than me for good advice.

I've done the same with qualities I've wanted to develop, like patience. "What would Mother Theresa do now?" I asked many years ago. Mother Theresa wouldn't shout! She wouldn't lose her cool. She'd send loving kindness and smile. And that's what I did whenever I got frustrated.

Coco Chanel was super smart! I have applied the strategies I'm sharing with you in my own life—personally and professionally.

If you've been procrastinating, experiencing self-doubt, feeling fearful, or just getting in your own way, you're in good company, Coco's been there. I've been there too—as have many successful people. Guess what, getting in your own way is normal!

I promise there are solutions to the problems you're currently facing—and you'll find them in the pages that follow.

Dig into this book and let Coco Chanel be your mentor, inspiration and guide as she calls forth your passions, purpose and potential.

Through the teachings of Coco, extensive research into the mysteries of motivation, success and fulfillment, and my own personal experience and professional success with clients as a holistic therapist, *Anxiety Rescue* will help you accelerate success. Together, Coco and I will guide you to where you need to go next, and give you practical steps to achieve success.

Like Coco Chanel I wasn't encouraged to pursue my natural inclination. My hope is that after reading this book you will be!

Whether your calling is the world of fashion, commerce, or seeking answers in the stars, it's never too late to be yourself.

Step into this ride joyfully and start creating your best life today.

PRINCIPLE ONE: THE CALL FOR SUCCESS

WHAT IS SUCCESS?

*There are people who have money
and people who are rich.*

~ Coco Chanel

Success is hard to define but easy to see and feel when you have achieved it. Being successful isn't necessarily about how much money you have, how many homes you own, or any of the other things people consumed with material possessions covet.

Being successful for increasing numbers of people includes: maintaining good health, energy and enthusiasm for life, fulfilling relationships, creative freedom, well-being, peace of mind, happiness and joy. Success also includes the ability to achieve your desires, whatever these may be, and being true to yourself.

Coco Chanel once said, "How many cares one loses when one decides not to be something but to be someone."

When you commit to being the creator of your life, and defining success on your own terms, you choose your '*someone.*' You will create and narrate the story of your life—just as Coco did.

YOUR CHALLENGE

What does success mean to you?

How will you know when you have succeeded?

Who are you, or will you, become?

What will the first line be in the story of your life?

> *The privilege of a lifetime is being who you are.*
>
> ~ Joseph Campbell, author

FOLLOW YOUR PASSION

Passion goes. Boredom remains.

~ Coco Chanel

Coco Chanel's extraordinarily passionate nature, and her ambitious quest for success drove and sustained her throughout her life and career.

She once said, "To be irreplaceable you have to be different." This is where following your soul's code, and living and working with passion comes in.

Passion is a source of huge energy from your soul that enables you to produce extraordinary results. Remarkable people get noticed and find life interesting.

- Passion helps people lead bigger lives
- Passion is an indispensable part of success
- Passion helps people achieve
- Passion energizes people
- Passion liberates people

- Passion allows people to be themselves
- Passion opens up fresh horizons
- Passion is good for health and helps people live longer.

YOUR CHALLENGE

What will passion do for you?

Be passionate in all that you do.

> *My intuition, my intention and my passion have allowed me to be who I am and will take me to higher ground.*
>
> ~ Oprah Winfrey, businesswoman

IF YOU NEED MORE help finding and living your passion my book, *Find Your Passion and Purpose: Four Easy Steps to Discover A Job You Want And Live the Life You Love*, will help. Available as a paperback, audio and ebook from all good online stores.

Or, you may prefer to take my online course, and watch inspirational and practical videos and other strategies to help you to fulfill your potential.

Click here to enroll or find out more—the-coaching-lab.teachable.com/p/follow-your-passion-and-purpose-to-prosperity

REALITY CHECK

Success is often achieved by those who don't know that failure is inevitable.

~ Coco Chanel

Pursuing and sustaining passion-driven success is not always fun. Like anything worthwhile, following your passion often involves great commitment, hard work and sacrifice.

Passionate people are prepared to give up things to live a more interesting life—Netflix, lounging on the sofa and indulging in a life of excess are just some of things that come to mind.

Passionate people are prepared to take risks and cope with failure. But the compensation is a bigger, fuller, more significant life with drive and purpose.

YOUR CHALLENGE

What are you prepared to trade-off to be more passionate?

What are you prepared to change in your life?

What would stop you?

What, or who, would sustain your quest for success?

> *I have learned throughout my life as a composer chiefly through my mistakes and pursuits of false assumptions, not by my exposure to founts of wisdom and knowledge.*
>
> ~ Igor Stravinsky, composer

BARKING UP THE WRONG TREE

*Luxury must be comfortable,
otherwise it is not luxury.*

~ Coco Chanel

Are you chasing the right dream? The ultimate luxury many people say, including Coco Chanel, is to become, who and what you really desire. But many people trade off their deeper passions for material comforts and status that can only ever give fleeting satisfaction.

Others lose their sense of self, trade their Integrity, smother their personality, and set fire to their relationships, chasing success at all costs.

Coco Chanel once said that one of her biggest regrets is that she didn't spend more time devoting herself to love—instead she chased the wrong dream.

Outwardly, people barking up the wrong tree appear successful but in fact they are deeply unfulfilled. As Coco Chanel once said, "A simple life, with a husband and children—a life with people you love—that is the real life." It's something she never achieved.

YOUR CHALLENGE

Are you chasing the right dream?

When you achieve success will you be happy with the person you've become?

Will any sacrifices you've made be worth it?

Are you ready for the day that we prayed for—already holding what is real. You know, the soul will find its own evolution and this is the only love that is real. And I tell you, I am keeping up the strength—you know I've got to try.

~ Barbara Streisand, singing 'Come Tomorrow'

REALIZE YOUR POTENTIAL

*In order to be irreplaceable
one must always be different.*

~ Coco Chanel

A life of no regret—isn't that what we all want? In my professional practice as a holistic psychologist and career coach so many people have told me they wished they had followed their passion and seized opportunities earlier, but that they lacked the courage to follow their convictions.

Often they wait to be pushed before they make the leap toward realizing their potential.

Abraham Maslow theorized in his infamous hierarchy of needs that becoming a self actualized person was the driving ambition and purpose of life. The ultimate success, he claimed, was to be all that you are capable of becoming.

Mademoiselle Coco Chanel threw herself into this quest with audacious determination. She vowed not to settle for the life she was born into.

Instead she devoted herself to realizing her potential. With ferocious willpower she aligned with the people who could elevate her success. How else could an impoverished orphan defy her origins and soar to eternal glory?

To fulfill her potential Coco Chanel continually reinvented herself. Success equalled growth, aligning with her heart's desire, and taking inspired action.

Being true to your self, and honoring the passion of your soul, can be the most beautiful feeling of all.

YOUR CHALLENGE

Are you ready to reinvent your life and achieve your greatest potential?

Or are you too comfortable—stagnating, not growing, nor challenging or exciting yourself?

Perhaps it's the fear of the unknown, or starting over, failing or succeeding. Fear is part of the human condition. It reminds you you're alive. It doesn't have to stop you from succeeding.

How could gaining more self-mastery benefit your life and boost your success?

Don't settle for okay.

> *You must learn to follow your destiny, whatever it maybe, with joy. As flowers grow they show off their beauty and are appreciated by all; then, after they die, they leave their seeds so that others may continue God's work.*
>
> ~ Paulo Coelho, author in his book, *The Spy*

LIVE AND WORK WITH PURPOSE

*Fashion has two purposes: comfort and love.
Beauty comes when fashion succeeds.*

~ Coco Chanel

Mademoiselle Chanel built a career on refashioning women's ideas of themselves. Liberating women from the confines of restrictive corsets and socially sanctioned norms about what was acceptable attire gave her a definitive life purpose. Her life's mission was to create more love, beauty and joy in women's lives and in those who loved them.

Everything she committed to achieve was done with purpose.

Given that you spend so much of your life working and you're living longer too, it's even more important to pursue your calling. Need convincing?

Benefits of working and living with purpose include:

- Tapping into your life's purpose gives you an edge, firing the flames of passion, enthusiasm, drive and initiative needed to succeed

- A sense of purpose can give you the courage, tenacity and clarity of vision needed to thrive
- Purpose fuels the embers of flagging motivation and helps fuel latent dreams
- A sense of purpose can lead you to the work you were born to do
- Discovering your true calling opens you up to the dreams the Universe has for you—bigger than you can dream for yourself.

YOUR CHALLENGE

What life experiences give you meaning and purpose?

How could your purpose benefit you and others?

It is in giving that I connect with others, with the world and with the divine.

~ Isabel Allende, author

IF YOU NEED MORE help finding your life purpose my book, *Find Your Passion and Purpose: Four Easy Steps to Discover A Job You Want And Live the Life You Love*, will help. Available as a audiobook, paperback and ebook from all good online stores.

PRINCIPLE TWO: EMPOWER YOUR SUCCESS

DREAM BIG

I invented my life by taking for granted that everything I did not like would have an opposite, which I would like.

~ Coco Chanel

In the movie, 'The Pursuit Of Happiness,' Will Smith, who plays the role of a homeless man, says to his son, "You got a dream, you gotta protect it. People can't do something themselves, they wanna tell you that you can't do it. You want something? Go get it. Period."

As a child Coco dreamed big. The flames of her desires were in part fueled by reading romance novels full of dashing heroes and heroines living absurdly, audaciously opulent and liberated lives.

I'm sure plenty of people tried to sabotage Coco's dreams of success—but she dreamed big dreams anyway. She knew that reality was a matter of perception, and once said that she would pretend she didn't hear people who criticized her, and could not see people with whom she disagreed.

Her strong will, boundless imagination, strength of purpose and courageous spirit are an inspiration to young and old.

People, impatient to see the realization of your dreams may say, "Show me the money" or "You've left it too late," or some other downer message.

Ignore them.

"It's already been done," people said to Tim Ferris when he shared his idea of starting a podcast. Instead of letting others talk him out of starting his show he did it anyway.

His podcast is now ranked #1 business podcast on all of iTunes, and it's been ranked #1 on numerous occasions. It is the first business/interview podcast to pass 100,000,000 downloads. It was also selected as iTunes' "Best of 2014" and "Best of 2015." Tim Ferris has also been called "the Oprah of radio".

YOUR CHALLENGE

Dream big. Everything starts as someone's daydream.

Fuel your verve—pursue the vision that sparkles.

Become audaciously obsessed.

Dream big but plan small. Baby steps will lead to bigger success.

Anchor your dreams within your heart and feel as though they are already achieved.

Create a soundtrack to feed your dreams. I still love Miley Cyrus's, *The Climb*, particularly the encouraging lyrics to persist and persevere. "Ain't about how fast I get there Ain't about what's waiting on the other side It's the climb."

Remember, you go where your vision is. Think Big, feel big, and know in your heart that you are one with God, and you will project a radiance, a glow, a confidence, a joy, and a healing vibration which bless all who come within your orbit now and forevermore.

~ Joseph Murphy, PhD, author and New Thought minister

PERFUME YOUR LIFE

*A women who doesn't
wear perfume
has no future.*

~ Coco Chanel

After the death of her playboy lover, Boy Chapel, Chanel became the mistress of the Russian Grand Duke Dmitri. Through him, she met Ernest Beaux, an expert perfumer whose father had worked for the Russian Czar.

Beaux was working on an essence for the French perfume maker François Coty. According to legend, after sampling the scent, Chanel made a few suggestions, then convinced Beaux to give it to her.

In 1924 she released it as Chanel N°5. It was the first perfume ever to bear a designer's name. She boldly advertised it as "A very improper perfume for nicely brought-up ladies."

The dark, leathery, distinctly masculine blend in its Art Deco bottle proved to be liquid gold.

With an uncannily knack of marketing nouse Coco quickly recognized the power of wooing Hollywood stars. When screen siren Marilyn Monroe was asked, "What do you wear to bed?" she famously answered, "Why, Chanel N°5, of course." Coco's fortune was made.

The transcendent alchemy of the potions that went into this formula were not left to chance. Grieving after Boy Chapel's death, Jasmine, Ylang Ylang, Vetiner and other restorative scents imbued Chanel N°5 with hope, healing, and the sensual confidence that love lost would be found again.

Aromatherapy, using the scents of plants and flowers, is one of many ancient remedies validated by modern science today. It's the Swiss army knife of all things healing—physically, mentally, spiritually and emotionally.

YOUR CHALLENGE

Investigate the power of smell. What scents imbue you with confidence?

Create your own success blend or have an expert create one for you. Beginning with how you want to feel is a good place to start.

I live to succeed.
Not to please you
or anyone else.

~ Marilyn Monroe, actress

YOUR SUCCESS NUMBERS

I'm presenting my dress collection on the 5th of May, the fifth month of the year.

~ Coco Chanel

You may believe in lucky numbers or you may call it superstition but many clever minds, including Einstein, Leonardo da Vinci and ancient philosophers revered the science and sacred mysteries of numerology.

Coco Chanel believed so strongly in the power of the number five she named her perfume, Chanel N°5 after it. Chanel N°5 is still a world favorite nearly one hundred years after its conception.

She knew the numerological significance of the number five, as representative of the fifth element—the legendary *quinta essential* of the alchemists: the Classical quintessence of which the cosmos is made.

Coco's interest in the language and magic numbers was also sparked during her time amongst the nuns.

At the age of twelve, Chanel was handed over to the care of nuns, and for the next six years spent a stark, disciplined existence in a convent orphanage, Aubazine, founded by Cistercians in the 12th century.

From her earliest days, the number five had potent associations for her. The paths that led Chanel to the cathedral for daily prayer were laid out in circular patterns repeating the number five.

Her affinity for the number five co-mingled with the abbey gardens, and by extension the lush surrounding hillsides abounding with cistus, a five-petal rose.

In 1920, when presented with small glass vials containing sample scent compositions numbered 1 to 5 and 20 to 24 for her assessment, she chose the fifth vial.

Chanel told her master perfumer, Ernest Beaux, whom she had commissioned to develop a fragrance with modern innovations: "I present my dress collections on the fifth of May, the fifth month of the year and so we will let this sample number five keep the name it has already, it will bring good luck."

For Coco, the number five was especially esteemed as signifying the pure embodiment of a thing, its spirit, its mystic meaning.

She was in good company along with Leonardo da Vinci she was guided by the sacredness of numbers and divine proportion some of the world's most enduring sacred monuments and successful brands dedicated to worship, beauty, and excellence have been inspired by a devotion to number.

YOUR CHALLENGE

Look deeper into the world of numbers and proportion and discover their secret mysteries.

What numbers are significant to you? What numbers might herald your success?

Without mathematics there is no art.

– Fra Luca Bartolomeo de Pacoli, mathematician

STAY SPARKLY

You can be gorgeous at thirty, charming at forty, and irresistible for the rest of your life.

~ Coco Chanel

"Don't let anyone dull your sparkle," writes psychologist and angel believer Doreen Virtue, in her book of the same name.

Despite the darkness of her childhood Coco Chanel lived a very sparkly life. She used an eclectic array of strategies to maintain her sparkle. Including designing and surrounding herself with things that gave her joy.

In her Parisian apartment a chandelier designed by her was adorned with dozens of crystal orbs and stars, camellias and grapes.

As Justine Picardie writes in her excellent book, *The Legend and The Life*, "Hidden letters and numbers in the black wrought-iron frame begin to emerge: G's for Gabrielle, Chanel's name at christening; double C's for Coco Chanel, the name under which she became famous; and fives—the number which made her a fortune, as the label on the perfume that still sells more than any other brand in the world."

To break free of negativity and drama Chanel would retreat to her beautiful apartment in the Ritz and look at the symbols and reminders that provided meaning to her life and sustained her—including simple white camellias that gave her so much joy.

The white camellia is rich with symbolism—it speaks to the heart and expresses positive feelings. It's most common meanings are:

- Desire or passion
- Refinement
- Perfection and excellence
- Faithfulness and longevity.

These meanings were all very central to Coco's philosophy of life and career success.

YOUR CHALLENGE

How can you break free of negativity and drama?

What, or who, can you surround yourself with to fill you with more joy?

How can you stay irresistible for the rest of your life?

What symbols reinforce what's most important to you?

If you are unhappy with anything…whatever brings you down, get rid of it. When you are free, your true creativity, your true self comes out.

~ Tina Turner, singer

DRESS JOYFULLY

The grand problem, the most important problem, is to rejuvenate women. To make women look young. Then their outlook changes. They feel more joyous.

~ Coco Chanel

Coco was a trailblazer in women's fashion. When she arrived in trousers in Venice people were shocked, but shock quickly turned to awe. Women wanted what she had—and Coco was only too happy to sell it to them.

Her joyous color was black. She loved its simplicity and understated elegance. Perhaps it reminded her of the habits the nuns, who so tenderly cared for her, wore.

Whatever the catalyst was, Coco had the vision to turn black, the color of mourning, into the symbol of independence, freedom, and strength. She also created the now iconic little black dress!

Your joyous color may be yellow, blue, or gold. Or it may be multi-patterned and have all the colors of the rainbow. Floating dresses in the finest silk may instill you with confidence, or perhaps you prefer something more tailored.

Whatever your color, whatever you wear, be sure that it makes you feel joyful.

YOUR CHALLENGE

Act as if. Take a job or lifestyle idea you are considering, or have always wondered what it would be like, and act as if you are living that role. Dress the part.

Have your colors professionally confirmed by a trained image consultant—when you dress in the colors that suit your skin tone you'll look younger and feel fabulous.

Dress shabbily and they remember the dress; dress impeccably and they remember the woman.

~ Coco Chanel

KEEP LEARNING

*I would make a very bad dead person,
because once I was put under, I would grow restless and would think only
of returning to earth
and starting all over again.*

~ Coco Chanel

Maintaining a commitment to lifelong learning—gaining new knowledge and new skills—is an important component of success.

Many personal and business failures can be attributed to not keeping abreast of trends, failing to adapt to changing landscapes, and misguided complacency.

Whether you succeed or not is as much about your willingness to start from the beginning, shear a path through the unknown, and what you learn along the way—including what to do and what not to do. But some people fear learning. They fear not being regarded as excellent in their field—*immediately*. Others fear being exposed as someone who doesn't have all the answers, making mistakes, and failing.

Coco Chanel wasn't born knowing how to be a hat designer, nor how to make clothes, nor how to run a business—especially in a terrain dominated by men.

Her commitment to acquiring knowledge, and willingness to learn from others as well as her own trial and error lead to her great accomplishments.

Learning through experience also lead to some of her biggest lessons—some of which cost her dearly.

For example, with the benefit of hindsight she wished she'd never gone into partnership with Alain and Gerard Wertheimer to produce and distribute Chanel N°5.

Coco spent many years locked in an acrimonious battle to gain a fairer portion of the profits of the perfume she created.

YOUR CHALLENGE

How can you embrace continual learning?

Who for what could be your greatest teacher?

How can you stay restless for new knowledge?

Learn to work harder on yourself than you do on your job. If you work hard on your job you can make a living, but if you work hard on yourself you'll make a fortune.

~Jim Rohn, author

PRINCIPLE THREE: EMPOWER YOUR VISION

STAY TRUE TO YOUR VISION

I wanted to give a woman comfortable clothes that would flow with her body. A woman is closest to being naked when she is well-dressed.

~ Coco Chanel

As Adam Markel writes in his book, *Pivot: The Art and Science of Reinventing Your Career and Life*, "Just because you can't see the steps doesn't mean they aren't there. There's a word for this type of behavior. It's called faith." This faith is shaped by gaining clarity about your purpose in life, he says

Coco's vision, and her resultant success, was clearly fueled by a strong sense of purpose. She wanted to unbind women from their corsets, to free them from restrictions, to liberate them from bondage. And she did this by creating clothes that empowered.

Before embarking on your visionary journey, you need to let go of "The Plan," and needing to have concrete guarantees before taking your first steps. You also need to disconnect from your ego and connect to God source, Markel says.

No doubt this was in part how Coco achieved her success. The seeds were planted when she was born to a seamstress mother, and blossomed in the orphanage where she learned how to sew.

More steps unfolded when she was drawn by the wonderful costumes in a local cabaret, and first enchanted Etienne Balsan, the wealthy man who would become her benefactor, with her beauty and voice. She left Etienne for one of his even wealthier friends, Arthur "Boy" Capel. Both men were instrumental in Chanel's first fashion venture.

Opening her first shop on Paris's Rue Cambon in 1910, Chanel started out designing and selling hats. She later added stores in Deauville and Biarritz and began making clothes. Her first taste of clothing success came from a dress she fashioned out of an old jersey on a damp dull day. So many people asked her where she got the dress from she offered to make one for them.

"My fortune is built on that old jersey that I'd put on because it was cold in Deauville," she once told author Paul Morand.

Further opportunities (and tragedies) unfolded, guiding her step-by-step toward her destiny. For example she only encountered the perfume expert who would later make her famous, when she went on a retreat to grieve the tragic death of her lover.

Importantly, while she had a clear purpose guiding her vision, she was quick to act on opportunities as they presented.

YOUR CHALLENGE

What are you clinging to that's preventing your from seeing your potential clearly?

How can you fortify your faith in your own vision, beliefs and goals and stick to them.

Be your own cheerleader and do not wait for approval nor support from others, listen to your gut and go for it.

Live your own truths and don't be challenged or coerced into conforming—it's all about your life path and rediscovering your power.

Following your dreams is not always practical, but not impossible. Most are attainable to some degree— it's always fantastic to feel that your vision is being pursued in some way and not buried and forgotten.

*The only thing worse than being blind
is having sight but no vision.*

~ Helen Keller, author

AWAKEN THE SEER

If you were born without wings, do nothing to prevent them from growing.

~ Coco Chanel

Several years ago when I was in New York I stumbled on a book that was to change my life—*Psychic Living: Tap into Your Psychic Potential*, by Andrei Ridgeway.

"In this technological day and age filled with busywork," Ridgeway writes, "many of us neglect our psychic potential. Our instincts are repressed and our inner voices buried.

"For many people, the word 'psychic' is so titanic, they can't accept it. They don't realize it's a normal state of being, that as a lover, and a friend, we use this part of ourselves all the time," Ridgeway writes.

Some people claim Coco Chanel was intuitive to the point of being psychic. She could see into the future, spot needs for which there would be later demand, and had a brilliant knack for creating the right product at the right time.

Some ways to awaken your psychic potential include:

- Meditation
- Yoga
- Aromatherapy
- Mindfulness
- Prayer
- Heart-based spiritual practices
- Free-writing/journalling
- Reading oracle or tarot cards—something Coco did regularly

YOUR CHALLENGE

How could you awaken or strengthen your psychic potential?

Engage all your senses so you can feel, taste, touch, smell and hear your future.

I have always been able to see what others were unable to see; and what they did, I did not see.

~ Salvador Dali, artist

REINVENT YOUR LIFE

I invented my life by taking for granted that everything I did not like would have an opposite, which I would like.

~ Coco Chanel

I hope that the quote above is as timely reminder for you, as it is for me, that you can transcend the things you dislike and create a life that fills you with joy—no matter what seemingly insurmountable obstacles block your path.

Barry Gibb, one of the members of the British group The Bee Gees, once said, "To go forward, you've got to be unsatisfied."

Clarifying your disappointments and intensifying your desires is an important part of gaining insight about what needs to change. An effective way to do this is to draw up a 'hello, goodbye list'.

Take a blank page and divide it into 3 columns. In the first column list all the things you want to leave firmly in the past. Head this 'goodbye.' Head the next column 'hello' and list all the things that you want to manifest. In the next column list all the benefits that acting on your 'goodbyes' and 'hello's' will give you.

One of my clients, Margaret, tried this strategy, and it worked fabulously. Feeling in a rut and lacking any clarity about what she wanted to do with the rest of her life she came to me for help.

"What am I going to say to Cassandra," she asked herself as she walked up to the office. She needn't have worried—the fact is that most clients have the solutions to their problems already. I just help tease them out.

After staring at the blank page for a period, her 'hellos' sprouted forth like dormant seeds waiting for the right fertilizer.

Margaret's 'hellos' included: "to follow my heart not my head, to use my skills in a more creative way, take up acting, increase my confidence and self esteem, spend quality time with my partner."

Margaret's goodbyes included, "goodbye to working for The Government and feeling suffocated in their overly structured, bureaucratic, rule bound ways of working; being stuck in an office environment; negative thoughts, being scared about leaving my job and not taking action toward my dreams."

How do you think acting on these intentions would benefit Margaret's life? Here are just a few she identified: "increased joy, lightness, energy, feeling more expansive and confident, growth, focus, calm & strength, identifying & achieving a new career path which is more in tune with my creative, innovative self and which allows me to use my gifts and favorite skills."

YOUR CHALLENGE

Reinvent your life. Take the negatives and transform them into positive intentions. Create your own 'hello goodbye list', including the benefits you will feel when you've make the changes.

Choose always the way that seems the best, however rough it may be. Custom will soon render it easy and agreeable.

ANXIETY RESCUE

~ Pythagoras, mathematician

BOOST YOUR MOTIVATION

A girl should be two things: classy and fabulous.

~ Coco Chanel

Being motivated predicts career success better than intelligence, ability, or salary—and there's plenty of research to prove it. Dan Ariely is a professor of behavioral economics at Duke University and the New York Times bestselling author of *Predictably Irrational* and *Payoff: The Hidden Logic That Shapes Our Motivations*.

To boost your motivation he suggests:

1) Focus On The Meaning In What You Do

"The things that give us deep happiness are inherently things that take longer and have a big element of meaning in them," he says.

Dan Pink, author of the bestseller *Drive: The Surprising Truth About What Motivates Us*— says these meaningful things give us purpose. And research shows purpose is one of the most powerful motivators there is.

Purpose, he says is, "Am I doing something in service of a cause larger than myself, or, at the very least, am I making a contribution in my own world?"

2) Take Ownership

If the task you have to do doesn't seem meaningful Pink suggests reframing your experience. "You might not be able to change what you have to do but you can change how you see it. And when you look at it through the lens of how it can help others, you'll often find more motivation."

Gabrielle Chanel was fiercely motivated to make something of her life. She used to toil for hours in the orphanage. She wouldn't allow herself to complain or become disillusioned that this was her lot. That frail, young girl would fiercely scowl at anybody who thought her destiny stopped there.

Her mindset wasn't "I'm slaving away, working for free, wasting my life." In her mind she wasn't forced to darn and sew. Her frame was, "I'm learning new skills and sending love into the world." And she never lacked for motivation.

When you feel connected to what you're doing, when you make something your own, you're naturally going to be much more motivated. Autonomy fuels your motivation, as it did Coco's, because, rather than feel you're a slave, you're self-directed. You've claimed some sovereignty over what you do, when you do it, how you do it.

3) Feel "The Intrinsic View"

Remind yourself of the intrinsic joy and positive emotions you feel while completing tasks. This is super powerful when you add to it the feeling of completion.

Often it's just a matter of what part of the activity you focus on before you start a task. Scientific studies shows exercise is one of the most beneficial activities to boost feelings of happiness. Yet so many of us avoid it. Why? Studies show that's because we focus on the beginning of the workout—the most unpleasant part.

If you think about the middle of the workout when you're feeling in the zone, you get the advantage of the intrinsic view and you're more motivated.

You could also project yourself to that amazing feeling of accomplishment you'll have after you've finished.

YOUR CHALLENGE

How can you reframe any doubts or fears, or disillusionment about your current situation to keep your motivation levels high?

How can you boost motivation and overcome procrastination by feeling 'the intrinsic view'?

> *Great things are not done by impulse but by a series of small things brought together.*
>
> ~ Vincent van Gogh, artist

MASTER THE ELEMENTAL ART OF SIMPLICITY

Elegance is refusal.

~ Coco Chanel

The convent abbey known as Aubazine where Chanel grew up was founded in the 12th century by the saint Étienne d'Obazine, as his name was rendered in Latin.

The saintly Etienne had a keen sense of its aesthetics during a period when Western cultural ideas about beauty and proportion were in radical transition.

He and the monks who followed him to this wilderness in a remote corner of south-western France were members of a new and rapidly growing Cistercian clerical order, which prized nothing so much as a life and an art of elemental simplicity.

These were formative years—shaping and crafting what would later become Coco Chanel's point of difference—austere grandeur. With her pared back designs, reverence for the simplicity and purity of the colors black and white, and exclusive focus on all things fashion, she proved less really can be more.

CASSANDRA GAISFORD

We live in an increasingly complicated and cluttered world. If overwhelm or chaos is getting you down it may be time to revisit simpler times. Say no to clutter, no to overload—no to anything that smothers the virtuosity of simplicity.

YOUR CHALLENGE

How can you simplify your life?

What does austere grandeur look like to you?

How will you feel when you have gained freedom from complexity?

Consider working with a clutter coach.

Boil it down to what counts most.
What is the most important thing? Things only get complicated when you are trying to address
too many issues.

~ Audrey Hepburn, actress

MAKE A PASSION ACTION PLAN

Beauty begins the moment you decide to be yourself.

~ Coco Chanel

Some people think that fate will take care of their future. The winners in life know that failing to make plans is committing to a plan of failure to make your dreams come true.

Instead, success in life is a mixture of good luck and skillful planning. Written goals, with action points and time frames are essential if you really want to achieve a more passionate life.

Of course, not everyone agrees. As you read earlier, some transformational change experts advocate letting things unfold.

It's a balancing act. Only you will know what helps you and what holds you back. And very often the task at hand will determine just how detached you can be.

It's hard to imagine Coco preparing for a collection without a finely executed plan of delivery. So if you are a 'go with the flow' type and aren't getting the results you desire, quit beating on the 'no planning wall' and find the door to your success.

YOUR CHALLENGE

Fuel your burning desire—make a passion action plan. Create a definite outline for carrying out your desire, and begin at once whether you are ready or not, to put it into motion.

Write out a clear, concise statement of your desired state. Read your written statement allow, twice-daily, once just before retiring at night, and once after rising in the morning. As you read it, see and feel and believe yourself already in possession of your desire.

Do something everyday to help move you closer to your goal of leading a more passionate life.

Don't forget to tick off and celebrate your achievements along the way to reinforce feelings of success.

> *You may say that it is impossible for you to 'see yourself in possession of money' before you actually have it. Here is where a burning desire will come to your aid. If you truly desire money so keenly that your desire is an obsession, you will have no difficulty in convincing yourself that you will acquire it. The objective is to want money, and to become so determined to have it that you convince yourself you will have it.*
>
> ~ Napoleon Hill, author

AFFIRM THAT YOU DESERVE SUCCESS

I don't do fashion, I AM fashion.

~ Coco Chanel

Mary Kay Ash, the founder Mary Kay Cosmetics, preached and practiced that the first step in achieving success is to firmly believe that you are an excellent person who deserves success. In Napoleon Hills's influential bestseller of all time, *Think and Grow Rich*, he shares some of her suggestions:

IMAGINE YOURSELF SUCCESSFUL. Always picture yourself successful. Visualize the person you desire to become. Set aside time each day to be alone and undisturbed. Get comfortable and relaxed. Close your eyes and concentrate on your desires and goals. See yourself in this new environment—capable and self-confident.

Reflect on your past successes. Every success, be it large or small, is proof that you are capable of achieving more successes. Celebrate each success. You can recall it when you begin to lose faith in yourself.

Set definite goals. Have a clear direction of where you want to go. Be aware when you begin to deviate from these goals and take immediate corrective action.

Respond positively to life. Develop a positive self-image. Your image, your reactions to life and your decisions are completely within your control.

YOUR CHALLENGE

What three things, if you changed them, would make a positive difference to your self-image, reactions to life and the impact of your decisions?

Our only limitations at those we set up in our own minds.

~ Napoleon Hill, author

PRINCIPLE FOUR: EMPOWER YOUR SPIRIT

SELF-RELIANCE

A woman needs independence from men, not equality. In most cases equality is a step down.

~ Coco Chanel

Coco learned from an early age that when all else fails, including the people that are meant to love and support you, you can always rely on yourself.

A singularly independent woman she was a trailblazer during a time when women were still largely dependent on their husband's.

However, in the early years of establishing her career she relied heavily on the good favor of wealthy men and saw purpose in being a kept woman until such time as she was able to maintain her independence. It was all part of her financial and personal freedom strategy.

YOUR CHALLENGE

How can you develop more self-reliance?

When you do spend time with others, choose carefully. Don't dilute your energy. Too much group think can stifle your confidence, motivation and originality.

Being solitary is not the same as being a loner. Learn from others but cultivate a good relationship with yourself.

Keep your own counsel.

If you are alone you belong entirely to yourself. If you are accompanied by even one companion you belong only half to yourself or even less in proportion to the thoughtlessness of his conduct.

~ Leonardo da Vinci, polymath

BELONG TO YOURSELF

As soon as you set foot on a yacht you belong to some man, not to yourself, and you die of boredom.

~ Coco Chanel

Coco Chanel was fiercely independent. This may be in part due to the wounds inflicted in her early childhood, by a father who reluctantly married her pregnant mother after Coco's birth, and later abandoned them all.

Some people fear success because they're afraid succeeding might mean having to choose work over intimate relationships. Others fear abandonment.

One of my clients only found her true groove in life when she left an unhealthy marriage—saving her career and her health in the process. Others have found their success is strengthened by the love and support of their significant other.

Only you can determine what your priorities are, how to balance competing demands on your time and energy and what you may, or may not, have to sacrifice. What matters most is maintaining a healthy self-esteem.

Healthy self-esteem means that you don't have to be in a relationship to feel love. You will always have the love you feel for yourself and (ideally) the love you feel for your work. You'll also attract love to you —the love and admiration of people who love you for you and for the contribution you make.

YOUR CHALLENGE

What beliefs do you have about success and relationships? How can you challenge these beliefs safely?

Who do you admire that works and lives with healthy self-love, regardless of others' value judgements?

Understand that the right to choose your own path is a sacred privilege. Use it. Dwell in possibility.

~ Oprah Winfrey, businesswoman

GET CREATIVE

*When I can no longer create anything,
I'll be done for.*

~ Coco Chanel

"Choose a job that allows the opportunity for some creativity and for spending time with your family. Even if it means less pay—it is better to choose work that is less demanding, that gives you greater freedom, more time to be with your family and friends, engage in cultural activities or just play. I think that is best," His Holiness, The Dalai Lama wrote in his book, *The Art of Happiness at Work*.

Not only do creative people get to do cool stuff, but creative people use their brains in the biggest way possible. They listen to and use both sides of their brains for maximum impact.

A few years ago, there was an article about the most desired recruits for medical school. Guess who they were? Students who were majoring in music. The reason was reported to be that their left and right brains are equally developed because music is mathematical and creative at the same time. The same point could be made for people who blend creativity with business—both draw on differing, but complementary, sides of the brain.

Creativity is also related to intuition—a powerful, non-rational innovative and decision making tool. More and more people and businesses are tapping into the power of intuition to help them achieve phenomenal results.

Powerful creativity is highly spiritual too. When you create your bring your whole soul into being and you enter a transcendental, meditative state. This state is something psychologist Mihaly Csikszentmihaly, refers to as 'flow.'

Natural abundance comes from "getting into the flow" by doing things that that bring feelings of inner excitement. The term, "follow your inner joy" is the key to abundance. Once you follow your inner most joy and adapt your situation to doing work that you love, then synchronicity begins to flow. This is the Universe's way of telling you that you are on the right track.

Daniel Pink, author of *A whole New Mind*, said, "The future belongs to a very different kind of person with a very different kind of mind—creators and empathizers, pattern recognizers and meaning makers. These people will now reap society's richest rewards and share its greatest joys."

Here's just a few things creativity can do for you:

- Increase your spiritual connection
- Enable you to access elevated levels of consciousness, higher imagination, intuition, the artistic level of the unconscious which is where the artist's magic lies
- Tap into your authenticity and true essence
- Relax your over-worked analytical mind
- Re-energize your flagging spirits
- Provide a wonderful escape from the 'real' world
- Encourage whole-braining learning
- Boost your intelligence and increase your likelihood of success.

CASSANDRA GAISFORD

YOUR CHALLENGE

When are the times you feel a sense of inner joy or flow?

How can you make more time for creativity?

How can you use creativity to solve a problem or challenge?

Art washes from the soul the dust of everyday life.

~ Pablo Picasso, artist

CHANGE YOUR NAME

My father was not there.

~ Coco Chanel

A radical change in name is one's commitment to a higher personal calling and is not uncommon among creative people, writes Twyla Tharp in *The Creative Habit: Learn It and Use It for Life.*

Used well a change of name can be globally memorable and a fulfilling prophecy of future success. Numerous people have achieved success writing under a pen name or pseudonym. Mozart played with multiple variations of his birth name most of his life. As did Marilyn Monroe and Coco Chanel—whose given name at birth was Gabrielle.

Coco Chanel's real name is as enigmatic as the lady herself—shrouded in mystery and cloaked in a layer of her own story-telling. One of the enduring mysteries surrounding Coco Chanel is exactly how she got her nickname. Some of her biographers go along with the story that her father nicknamed her "Coco."

Others contend that Chanel came by the name during her brief stint as a cabaret singer because her repertoire consisted of only two songs:

"Ko ko ri Ko" and "Quiqu `a vu Coco?" But according to one source, Chanel herself once explained that the name was nothing more than a shortened version of "coquette," the French word for "kept woman."

Coco rarely talked about the circumstances of her birth, but once said that she was named in part after one of the nuns in the hospital poorhouse for illegitimate children where she was born. The name of the nun was Gabrielle Bonheur, according to Chanel. However the name Bonheur does not appear on her baptismal certificate. Bonheur in french means 'happiness' and Coco may have created this story to lay claim to its meaning.

She was a child of the poorhouse, plain Gabrielle Chasnel (a version of her surname which also exists in historical records, and which she claims was an error). She remained Gabrielle for most of her childhood —the nickname "Coco" which she adopted, and for which she became famous, is also anchored in untruths regarding its origin. In some versions she says her father called her "Little Coco." because he never liked "Gabrielle."

It is said that she thought, 'Coco' was an awful name yet she was proud of its recognition throughout the world. The Infamous courtesan Mata Hari, was proud of her fame too. Her real name was Margaretha Zelle—later she was forced to adopt her married name MacLeod, before ditching them both to pursue independence (and infamy) as a dancer and courtesan in Paris.

Both women shared a tragic past from which they sough permanent escape, and both sought independence through fame. And both yearned to be loved.

Interestingly the name on Coco's tombstone she designed for herself simply says, 'Gabrielle Chanel.' It has a simple cross, and five lions heads.

YOUR CHALLENGE

How could you experiment with a new name and new identity?

How could 'hiding' behind a false name give you confidence and courage?

> *You're not a star until they
> can spell your name in Karachi.*
>
> – Humphrey Bogart, actor

PRAY

J'aime la vie! I feel that to live is a wonderful thing.

~ Coco Chanel

As Justine Picardie writes in her excellent book, *The Secret Life of Coco Chanel*, Chanel never admitted to her years at Aubazine, where she lived from the age of 11 to 18, in an orphanage run by the sisters of the Congregation of the Sacred Heart of Mary.

But the fact was that Coco spent much of her early years under the care of the Catholic nuns. Having been abandoned by her father, and knowing she was penniless, the ritual of prayer was a constant part of daily life, and a source of nourishment and filling her with the hope that her life would be beautiful.

"Prayer is when you talk to God; Meditation is when you listen to God," says author Diana Robinson. Others refer to the voice of God as tapping in to their intuition, higher self, inner goddess or Sacred Divine. Whatever your belief system, prayer is a form of spiritual communion.

Many people have lost their union with God because of the hypocritical dogma which has polluted many faith systems. As the author of *The Alchemist*, Paulo Coelho, shares on the back jacket of his book, *The Spy*—a fascinating story about Mata Hari, "He has experimented with magic and alchemy, studied philosophy and religion, read voraciously, lost and recovered his faith, and experience the pain and pleasure of love.

"In searching for his own place in the world, he has discovered answers for the challenges that everybody faces. He believes that within ourselves, we have the necessary strength to find our destiny."

One of the key tools that has given him strength is prayer. As he writes in the foreword to *The Spy*, "O Mary, conceived without sin, pray for us who have recourse to You. Amen."

"Scientific (4-step) prayer therapy is the only really answer to the great deception," writes Joseph Murphy (PhD.) in his excellent book, *The Miracle of Mind Dynamics*. "Let the light of God shine in your mind, and you will neutralize the harmful effects of the negatives implanted in your subconscious mind."

The four steps include:

1.) Recognition of the healing presence of Infinite intelligence

2.) Complete acceptance of the One Power

3.) Affirmation of the Truth

4.) Rejoice and give thanks for the answer

The indicator of God's presence in you is the presence of peace, harmony, abundance, and perfect health.

YOUR CHALLENGE

Embark on some scientific prayer therapy.

Take the time to stop and pray from your heart. The words that you use aren't as important compared to the strength of your desire to connect with The Divine.

Be open to a response appearing which is different from your expectations—and know that your prayers are heard and answered.

Faith is action in love.

~ Mother Theresa

MAINTAIN YOUR FAITH

I've done my best, in regard to people and to life, without precepts, but with a taste for justice.

~ Coco Chanel

If you read about the lives of men and women who have achieved success, you'll discover that maintaining their faith played a major role. Many times the results you want to achieve take time to appear. Without faith, doubts and disbelief can sabotage your chances of success. Getting discouraged, feeling pessimistic, or worse—giving up are some of reasons people fail.

"Faith is action in love and love is action in service," Mother Theresa once said. "By transforming that faith into living acts of love, we put ourselves in contact with God."

Coco Chanel was a woman of faith. She knew the power of cultivating and maintaining unwavering belief. Her faith was always driven by love. Love of the clothes she designed, love of the perfume she created, love of the people's lives she transformed—whether through her patronage or the things she made. And her faith was also driven by her passion for justice.

Faith is not always about spirituality or religion—faith can be about your belief in your ability to succeed. It's as much about your dedication to not be something, but to be someone—your glorious successful self!

Julia Cameron, an active artist and author of The *Artist's Way*, and another thirty or so fiction, and non-fiction books, advocates relinquishing too much effort and turning energy instead from one of stressful striving, to cultivating faith and trust.

Prayer, gratitude, acceptance and unwavering belief that everything happens for a reason, are just some of the many strategies she encourages people to embrace.

YOUR CHALLENGE

How can you maintain the faith? Stay positive and keep away from cynics. Tap into the awesome power of meditation, yoga and a spiritual faith based perspective to help you maintain a positive expectancy, manage stress and increase your intuitive, creative powers.

Empower your faith in your vision—visualize your goal as already achieved.

Empower your faith in yourself—create some affirming affirmations and say them regularly.

Be of service—transform your faith into living acts of love.

Identify some ways you can take action—even when you feel the odds are stacked against you, or you feel like giving up.

IF FAITH IS something you'd like to cultivate, you'll find them throughout my *Mid-Life Career Rescue* series. You may also like to check out Julia's book *Faith and Will*, or find your own sources.

To pray is to let go and let God take over.

~ Philippians 4:6-7

CONSULT THE ORACLES

*I don't care what you think about me.
I don't think about you at all.*

~ Coco Chanel

Tarot and other subjects such as astrology, alternative healing, psychic phenomena, spirituality, and a fascination with the Goddess captured Coco Chanel's interest.

As the astrologer Jessica Adams shares on her website,

> "Coco Chanel used the Lenormand oracle card deck to help her in business—as well as in her personal life. As my friend Justine Picardie explains in her acclaimed biography of Chanel, the cards still rest where she left them, lying in a moment frozen in time, in her apartment in Paris."

Coco was taught the precepts of theosophy by the first and foremost love of her life, the English playboy, Captain Arthur Edward "Boy" Capel (CBE). Theosophy is defined by some sources as, "A collection of mystical and occultist philosophies concerning, or seeking direct knowledge of, the presumed mysteries of life and nature, particularly of the nature of divinity and the origin and purpose of the universe."

My first experience with psychic phenomena and the tarot was when I was a teenager in New Zealand in the late 70s. A friend had given her baby up for adoption and asked me to come with her to visit psychic for a reading. I remember feeling both apprehensive and excited.

I was amazed that the reading revealed such true things about my life, and I knew there was something special about tarot cards.

Like Coco it's a fascination that stayed with me throughout my life and which continues to provide inspiration courage and fortitude—both personally and professionally. No one knows exactly how tarot cards originated. The earliest tarot deck dates back to the 1400s Renaissance Italy.

"Ive come to believe that a lot of wisdom was incorporated in the tarot. I feel, as do others, that ancient keepers of the old ways or earth-based spirituality wanted to pass on information," writes Karen Vogel in the introduction to her *Motherpeace Tarot Guidebook*.

> "As warfare increasingly became a way of life in the Dark Ages of Europe, old ways were lost as whole cities and civilizations were wiped out.
>
> It was more and more difficult to pass on oral and written traditions since whole cultures were destroyed and ancient libraries burned. One of the traditional stories about the origins of the tarot is that the wisdom keepers in these cultures were the storytellers, artists and healers.
>
> They chose between writing a spiritual or philosophical text or putting the knowledge into a game. They decided that a game in the form of cards would last longer, be more accessible to everyone, and easier to hide."

By the Renaissance, Christianity had dominated Europe as both a political and religious powerhouse. Millions of women, who were often the healers and spiritual leaders were murdered during the Inquisition.

Those who threatened Church authority or knew about ritual and healing, either died or when in hiding taking certain information with them. It was in this atmosphere that tarot began and subsequently spread all over Europe.

Like many people, Coco Chanel found great wisdom, peace, comfort and healing from an eclectic array of spiritual rituals.

Of all the psychological theories in the West, that of revered Swiss psychologist Carl Jung, stands out as most applicable to Tarot.

Jung wrote about Tarot on several occasions, seeing it as depicting archetypes of transformation like those he found in myths, dreams and alchemy.

He described its divination abilities as similar to the IChing and astrology, and late in life established a group who attempted to integrate insights about a person based on multiple divination systems including Tarot.

Jessica Adams also notes, "This connection with astrology is not something that the house of Chanel shies away from today. In fact, I vividly remember Karl Lagerfeld's illustration of the zodiac sign Sagittarius, decorating my horoscope column in Vogue Australia, when he became a Guest Editor at the end of the year."

Astrology also played a major role in Lagerfeld's *Chance* campaign—the Chanel-Leo is very important when understanding the house of Chanel, the woman who created it and the fragrance.

Jessica Adams also suggests that one of the cards in Coco's Lenormand deck inspired one of the secret ingredients contained in Chanel N°5, "…this card shows a beautiful green tree, seven love hearts and the message…'A tree far away means good health, when near, illness there will be, many trees close together means things will turn out all right, you'll see.'

As we now know, a naturally occurring tree moss is one of the secret ingredients in Chanel N°5 fragrance. A coincidence? Or did Chanel bring together astrology and the Lenormand, when choosing her blend?"

YOUR CHALLENGE

Experiment with tarot—either have a reading with an experienced tarot card reader, or study the cards and their meanings for yourself.

Feed your curiosity—take note of the places and circumstances where tarot, astrological symbols and other mystical and occultist philosophies are used—in business and life.

How could you blend astrology and tarot into your career and life?

> *He who has a mind to understand,*
> *let him understand.*
>
> ~ Mary Magdalene, in The Gospel of Mary

PRINCIPLE FIVE: EMPOWER YOUR MIND

FAITH IN YOUR STARS

Arrogance is in everything I do. It is in my gestures, the harshness of my voice, in the glow of my gaze, in my sinewy, tormented face.

~ Coco Chanel

Much of Coco Chanel's success can be attributed to her faith in the stars. Chanel believed in astrology. She was a Leo, symbolized by the lion, queen of the beasts, Leo is the sign of royalty. Proud and arrogant, yet loyal and brave, this sign if ablaze with warmth and fire.

Creative entrepreneurship is the true stamp of a Leo—and Chanel manifested this in buckets. Driven by passion, purpose, determination, a desire to lead not follow, the courage and fearlessness of a lion, and a serious need to be noticed. Making an impression is Priority One for many Leo's—think Mick Jagger, Arnold Schwarzenegger, Julia Child and other flamboyant people who share Coco Chanel's sun.

Chanel's moon was in Pisces, making her intuitive to the point of being psychic, writes Karen Karbo in *The Gospel According to Coco Chanel*. This may explain her uncanny knack for predicting where best to place her energy to amass a great following and fortune.

Leo is also the fifth sign of the zodiac—a number Coco used to astounding success when she named her perfume, Chanel No. 5. She also leveraged off her faith in her stars and other spiritual tools to empower her mind, and sustain her during periods of darkness.

"*Most clients come with financial problems or relationship problems,*" my friend and astrologer Marianne O'Hagan says. "They come looking for the hope of happiness in the future."

Marianne knows personally and professionally. You can read more of her story in Mid-Life Career Rescue: What Makes You Happy— including how she started her own business by using her faith in the stars.

I'm a Libra in Western astrology and a Snake in Chinese astrology. It's true when they say that Libran's love harmony, balance and beauty. I love it when I receive feedback from readers, saying my book is "beautifully written."

Or, as a person who read my first Art of Success book, inspired by Leonardo da Vinci book, posted in their review, "*This beautiful book wraps art around business and life and makes each hum with energy and creativity and brings the reader new vitality.*"

Google 'best careers' for Snakes and I'm told to avoid careers where I have to work too hard. 'Working hard' to me is doing something I dislike, working with people I don't respect. Working hard is not marching to my own beat. But when I'm working in the passion zone, fulfilling my purpose, now that's a different story.

Whether you're a believer in the notion that whatever planets align at your time and place of birth can determine your intrinsic strengths, shape your character, relationships and fortunes, there's plenty of helpful data to aid you in your quest for success. Keep an open mind and don't take everything as total gospel.

YOUR CHALLENGE

Go cosmic—gain additional insight about your astrological sign from any of the plethora of books, online resources and personal astrologers. Focus on identifying your strengths, Achilles heel, and best-fit-factors career-wise and in your personal life.

> *I liked the idea that astrology believes we all are special and have unique gifts. It was at that moment that my love of astrology was born.*
>
> ~ Marianne O'Hagan, astrologer

BOOST YOUR SELF-AWARENESS

I'm neither smart nor stupid, but I don't think I'm a run-of-the-mill person. I've been in business without being a businesswoman, I've loved without being a woman made only for love.

~ Coco Chanel

How can you be true to yourself if you don't know who you are and who you want to be?

Astrology is just one of many helpful tools to boost self-awareness. But very often it provides just a small part of the puzzle of discovering your authentic self.

Leonardo da Vinci once said, "The acquisition of knowledge is always of use to the intellect, because it may thus drive out useless things and retain the good."

While Leonardo clearly didn't have access to modern personality tests he was a master in the realms of observation. He knew what gave him energy, how he preferred to take in information, make decisions and organize his life.

The Myers Briggs Type Indicator is one of the most popular preference-based personality assessment tools. Experts differ in whether Leonardo's personality preferences were INTP (Introverted, Intuitive, Thinking, and Perceiving), or ISTP (Introverted, Sensing, Thinking, and Perceiving), or even an ENTP (Extroverted, Intuitive, Thinking, and Perceiving).

While guesswork is rarely accurate some people believe that Coco Chanel shared a similar personality to Leonardo—the main difference lay in her ability to plan, schedule and start and finish the projects she committed to—making her INTJ.

For more information about The Myers Briggs Type Indicator, turn to Google or consult a registered MBTI practitioner for an accurate assessment.

Neuropsychologist, Katherine Benziger says, "People are happiest, healthiest and most effective when developing, using and being rewarded for using their natural gifts." This is very true.

Paying greater attention to the things that stir you soul, ignite your passion, and awaken your heart are also great ways to boost your self-awareness.

YOUR CHALLENGE

Make boosting your self-awareness your priority. Who are you? What are your natural gifts? What are your super powers? How can you do and be what you are?

Keep a passion journal, and notice all the times, people and events that make your spirit soar

What comes naturally to you? What can you do without really *trying*?

Notice the times you feel marvelous.

The more you know about yourself the better your decisions will be. You'll also have better success in presenting yourself and your natural talents in the best light—to others and yourself.

Do you know what you are? You are a marvel. You are unique. In all the years that have passed, there has never been another child like you. Your legs, your arms, your clever fingers, the way you move. You may become a Shakespeare, a Michelangelo, a Beethoven. You have the capacity for anything. Yes, you are a marvel.

~ Pablo Picasso, artist

CREATE A NEW LIFE STORY

A girl should be two things: who and what she wants.

~ Coco Chanel

No one will ever know the real Coco Chanel, because she designed it that way. She once said, "People's lives are an enigma."

She perpetrated her own mystery by constantly creating a new life story, reinventing her past and weaving around and around her family history.

It wasn't a history she was proud of. She felt the stigma of her illegitimate birth in a poorhouse to parents who, for all intents and purposes, were wandering gypsies.

To live the fantasy that sustained her as a young girl locked in a convent she imagined a new life—and with it a new life story about her background.

She obscured her past from others, refashioning its heartaches and betrayals, smoothing away the rough edges. She reengineered her history just as she recut the sleeves of a dress, unfastening seams that pinched, cutting unsightly threads, and then sewing it back together.

She once said, "I don't like the family. You're born into it, not of it. I don't know anything more terrifying than the family…Childhood—you speak of it when you're very tired, because it's a time when you had hopes, and expectations."

Like real stories in books and movies, your life story will have a hero (you), a quest, obstacles to overcome to achieve the story goal and a climax—and hopefully, a happy ending.

YOUR CHALLENGE

Who are you? What's your story? We live the lives we imagine. Retell your story—leaving out the bits you don't want to relive.

If your childhood didn't meet your expectations, if your family or personal history feels like a hindrance, or if you are dragging around the baggage of a disappointing, hurtful or traumatic past—*act as if.*

Act as if you had a different past. Create a new historical account of the life you lived—as long as your intention is not to create fraud and ruin lives.

Rewrite your life story so that it becomes meaningful—leading to growth and transformation.

~ Catherine Ann Jones, author of Heal Your Self with Writing

ACCENT THE POSITIVE

There have been several Duchesses of Westminster but there is only one Chanel!

– Coco Chanel

Coco the Duke of Westminster enjoyed a decade-long love affair. Destined to be a lover and never a wife, she was said to have been devastated when the man she regarded as her greatest love, Boy Capel, married an English aristocrat, Lady Diana Wyndham. He was never faithful to her, or to anyone, and their affair continued after his marriage.

Coco always accented the positive—no matter how bitterly her heart was crushed. Whether it was ego, pride or with a practical realization that giving in to forlorn thoughts would never be a winning formula, Coco always modeled positivity.

When you let desire not fear propel you forward, magic happens. It's the Law of Attraction. The Law of Manifestation. The Law of Intention. But it only works if you stay positive. Negativity is a repellent. Positivity is a magnet, drawing abundance forward.

YOUR CHALLENGE

How can you stay positive even when things look bleak?

Set your horizons high, believe in the beauty of your dreams and don't settle for less.

Negative thoughts are like weeds—they grow untended, positive thoughts are like flowers —you need to nurture them every day.

~ His Holiness, The Dalai Lama

FAILURE IS NOT FATAL

Success is most often achieved by those who don't know that failure is inevitable.

~ Coco Chanel

Oprah Winfrey, once said, "I have a lot of things to prove to myself. One is that I can live my life fearlessly."

It's a sentiment Mademoiselle Chanel took to heart with the courage and fierce determination of Leo the Lion.

Although she is widely recognized as one of the world's greatest fashionistas, she also made colossal mistakes and suffered staggering failures which would have felled many.

But she persevered anyway. She knew that learning from her own experience also meant learning from her mistakes.

The French fashion press lay in wait for her first post-war collection," Justine Picardie writes in, *Coco Chanel: The Legend and The Life* "like cats at a rat hole."

Her desire to relaunch her career in American was a massive public failure. She had worked tirelessly on the collection, despite being ill with a stoppage in her intestine, so the damming reviews condemning her collection as 'a sad retrospective,' and 'a failure to engage with fashion,' were even more cruel. Other critics attacked her personally.

A woman less sure of herself would have been quit. But their attack only served to stir her fighting blood.

But she didn't put away her scissors, nor her inventor's hat. She never lost the courage to continue—driven by a determination for justice and to prove her critics wrong.

She learned from her failures, accepted them as par for the course, and continued her pioneering quest to learn, experiment and explore.

YOUR CHALLENGE

Are you prepared to fail in order to succeed? Do you give yourself permission to learn from mistakes?

What new experiences are you prepared to embark on?

What is the biggest mistake you ever made and what did you learn?

What would you do differently if you had no fear of making mistakes?

Whose failure story inspires you? Why? What does it teach you?

Reframe failure. The greatest lessons come not from your successes but from your failures. What can you let your failures teach you? Don't look at hurdles as a negative thing but as a reflective tool on how to improve.

Reading biographies of people like Coco Chanel and Leonardo da Vinci and other people whose success you admire can give you great encouragement along your path to creating your own victories.

Success is not final, failure is not fatal: it is the courage to continue that counts.

~ Winston Churchill, politician

MAKE MISTAKES

*I am continuing, I shall continue.
They'll end up understanding.*

~ Coco Chanel

So many people fear failing because they worry about what others may say about them if they don't succeed. Take a leaf from Coco's book of life—don't think about what they think at all!

It may be challenging, it may be easier said than done, but investing in strategies to care less about what others think and more about what you think about yourself will prove liberating. As Coco once said, "A girl should be two things: who and what she wants."

Sometimes the greatest fortune comes from making the biggest mistakes. Here's just a few mistakes that turned out well:

- The renowned Stradivarius violin became the world's finest and most costly musical instrument by mistake
- The modern pacemaker was born from an error by its

developer who inadvertently put the wrong sized resistor into his nascent heart rhythm device
- Charles Goodyear of tyre empire fame accidentally boiled a brew of rubber and sulfur. When he returned to his chemical stew he found a versatile new plastic
- Inventor Spencer Silver had been attempting to develop an ultra strength adhesive for 3M laboratories ,but instead developed a sticky substance that could easily be pulled off. His colleague Art Fry used the glue to hold his hymnbook bookmark in place and the first post-it was born
- Alexander Fleming left a number of laboratory petri dishes unwashed and returned to find that many of them had been contaminated and grown bacteria colonies. On one however he noted that a patch of mold had prevented the growth of bacteria which prompted him to explore the substance's bacteria-killing properties.
- Musician Ornette Coleman's mistake led him to be acclaimed as the inventor of 'free jazz.' He was awarded the MacArthur Fellowship (nicknamed the Genius Award) in 1994 and the Pulitzer Prize for Music in 2007.
- Coco Chanel's critics said she made a mistake when she attempted to relaunch her fashion house after the war. French and British journalists called her comeback collection, "A flop." Others, including the influential editor at Harpers Bazaar, Dianne Vreeland, ran front page spreads. Unexpected support from her business partner Wertheimer, also ended a three decade long feud.

But, still she continued.

YOUR CHALLENGE

Buoy your resolve by collecting stories about other people who were treated harshly by peers, critics, family and other disbelievers.'

Collect a file of inspiring stories about mistakes that turned out well.

Refuse to be a victim. Next time you feel you've made a mistake, ask yourself, "How could this work out for my highest good?" or "What can learn?'

Be gentle with yourself. Sometimes making mistakes heralds a time of new birth and energy. Draw on the lessons you have learned to help you move forward.

Notice how you have grown and changed as a result of everything that has happened.

Gather information as you go and be ready for a new adventure. Look for positive signs for successful outcomes in the future.

*It was when I found out I could make mistakes
that I knew I was on to something.*

~ Ornette Coleman, Musician

BOOST YOUR BELIEF

A woman needs independence from men, not equality. In most cases equality is a step down.

~ Coco Chanel

It's the messages you tell yourself that matter most, says celebrity Hypnotherapist and Author Marisa Peers. "Belief without talent will get you further than talent with no belief. If you have the two you will be unstoppable."

Coco Chanel believed from a very early age that the daughter her freedom and self respect lay in securing and maintaining her independence.

She also believed in the power of being loved as a woman. She had no desire to be a man—only to be loved by them. "A woman who is not loved is no woman", she once said.

Many people mistakenly sacrifice their relationships in pursuit of successful careers. Unhelpful beliefs, including, "You can't have it all" or, "You can't have a relationship and be successful," may partly be to blame.

You may not be aware of your own self-limiting beliefs and patterns, or the negative, confining impact of others' beliefs about what you should be doing with your life. Perhaps you've defined your life according to what others think you are capable of, or believe you should settle for.

Even when the answers are clear you may resist the changes needed to achieve more happiness and passion in your work or personal life. Fear often lies at the heart of this reluctance or resistance.

Viktor Frankl, a psychiatrist and survivor of the Nazi concentration camps, believes that the cause of people's fear is a basic and crippling lack of faith about themselves and their capacity to make positive and successful changes.

To get at some of the core beliefs standing between you and the success you desire ask yourself, "I'll do anything to achieve (insert goal/dream) just don't ask me to do that (insert the fear or belief that holds you back.)

Acknowledge the things you don't believe and challenge them. Interview your beliefs, by asking them the following questions.

- "Where's your evidence for that?" (That being what ever you fear or hold to be true?)
- "What's the worse that could happen if you pursued your passion? How bad would that really be? How can you increase the likelihood of success?"
- "What tells you that you could follow your dreams?" (a nice shift from focusing on the problem, to looking for solutions instead).
- "What have you tried recently that worked? What you are you doing now that works?"
- "Who do you know who is happy at work? What could you learn from them?"
- "How does your (supportive other) know you can do this? What difference will it make to them when you are happier?"

You'll find other helpful strategies to challenge self-limited beliefs in my book, *Boost Your Self-Esteem and Confidence: Six Easy Steps to Increase Self-Confidence, Self-esteem, Self-Value and Love Yourself More.*

I've also included a helpful section in my book, *Mid-Life Career Rescue: What Makes You Happy.* In this book I share my experience following reading, T*he Biology of Belief: Unleashing the Power of Consciousness, Matter & Miracles,* by Dr. Bruce Lipton.

YOUR CHALLENGE

So often we aren't even aware of what our self-limiting beliefs are. If your beliefs are ingrained, or you keep sabotaging your own success, seeking help from a qualified practitioner with expertise in reprogramming stubborn, disempowering beliefs may be a game-changer.

Chances are you don't need to see a therapist to move beyond self-limiting beliefs, but if you do, great. Go do it. There's magic in that.

You can also learn from some of the most powerful, effective and simple techniques used by practitioners working in the realm of positive psychology and mind reprogramming—including hypnosis

I told my audience that if they changed their beliefs they could change their lives.

~ Dr. Bruce Lipton , cell biologist

PRINCIPLE SIX: EMPOWER YOUR BODY

SHARPEN YOUR MOST POTENT TOOL WITH SCENT

Fashion is not something that exists in dresses only. Fashion is in the sky, in the street, fashion has to do with ideas, the way we live, what is happening.

~ Coco Chanel

Do you have the right attitude? Are you happy with your ideas and the way you live? Focus, motivation, sharpness and alertness—more than your skills or capabilities, it is your state of mind that determines how successful and happy you will be.

There are many ways to empower your mind—working with essential oils is one of the most effortless.

Coco Chanel knew the alchemical potency of flowers and plants. She surrounded her self with nature's elixir and amassed a fortune from the sales of her most famous perfume—Chanel N°5.

Here's a few essential oils and natural therapeutic remedies to lend your mind a helping hand:

1.) Laurel Essential Oil: Motivates people who lack energy or confidence. Strengthens the memory and helps maintain concentration, especially during prolonged tasks

2.) Rosemary Essential Oil: Instills confidence during periods of self-doubt and keeps motivation levels high when the going gets tough. It is also said to help maintain an open mind and to make you more welcoming of new ideas.

3.) Cardamom Essential Oil Stimulates a dull mind, dispels tensions and worries, and nurtures and supports the brain and nervous system. Many people find it of great support during challenging times.

4.) Peppermint Essential Oil: With its refreshing scent peppermint works like a power boost for your fatigued mind, making you feel more sharp and alert.

YOUR CHALLENGE

Read more about aromatherapy for achievers and learn about essential oils for success.

Sharpen your most potent tools—your heart and your mind. Become a perfumer—experiment with essential oils until you find a winning blend.

If you believe in aromatherapy… it works! If you don't believe in aromatherapy… it works!

~ Cristina Proano-Carrion, aromatherapist

RESTORE YOUR ENERGY

Those who create are rare; those who cannot are numerous. Therefore, the latter are stronger.

~ Coco Chanel

Coco loved her work, but she still made time to rest. Your physical and emotional health is better supported by investing in gentle rituals that restore and energize you.

Yet in today's world being busy is often worn like a "badge of honor," says author and nutritional biochemist, Dr Libby.

"Many people see rest as failure," she says. "However regularly finding space so that you can rest is one of the best health investments you can make.

If you are seeking permission to rest, or simply looking for some restorative strategies here are a few ideas to help you:

1.) Wake 30 minutes earlier than your household. While not technically resting, creating space for some morning rituals can create an unparalleled sense of calm. Rising earlier than everyone else will enable you to make the most of the peacefulness that morning can bring. Find a quiet spot and set your intentions for the day.

2.) You may also enjoy the art of writing morning pages. Julia Cameron, in her most excellent book *The Artist's Way* (a must buy), recommends writing morning pages everyday. The writing is just stream of consciousness, writing out whatever you are feeling—good (or what one of my clients calls the "sunnies") or not so good ("the uglies")

It's a way of clearing the mind—"a farewell to what has been and a hello to what will be," Julia says. "Write down just what is crossing your consciousness. Cloud thoughts that move across consciousness. Meeting your shadow and taking it out for a cup of coffee so it doesn't eddy your consciousness during the day."

3.) Pablo Picasso once said, "Art washes from the soul the dust of everyday life." Creating art can be a wonderfully meditative, tranquil practice. You work of art doesn't have to be brilliant, and you don't have to share it with the world. It doesn't even need to involve paint or canvas. It may be as simple as coloring in.

4.) Float. Artist Mark Olson cares for his body and soul by spending time in his personal flotation chamber (a light-and sound-proof tank filled with water) .

An added benefit of this gentle practice is that it provides him with further inspiration. You may not have access to a flotation chamber, but just soaking in some water can be hugely therapeutic.

5.) Meditate. It's a little like exercise," says British actor Jude Law. "It stops me overthinking and focuses my actions. What won me around was that I was in my early 40s and wasn't able to find 20 or 30 minutes a day just to sit and think.

"It seems appalling that out of the long day that something we find so hard to do and suddenly it became a necessity to leave all the stuff, not answer anything, just breathe and try to be."

6.) Improve your sleep. Many of us have little or no transition into rest, says Dr. Libby. "We simply put a head on the pillow and expect to switch off. A simple meditation focusing on your breath is a way to ease into rest.

"Lay on the floor, or on the bed, or sit supported in a chair, whatever you prefer. Bring your focus to your breath moving in and out of your nostrils," she says.

If you need additional help there are many wonderful guided meditation videos and audio is available online. Use these as a guide to help you find what works for you.

7.) Coco was a prolific reader and surrounded herself with books. There is often nothing more replenishing than a good read and introverted time spent by yourself can be incredibly restorative.

New research also suggests that reading books every day can help you live longer. A study published by US researchers in the academic journal Social Science & Medicine concluded that, "Book reading provides a survival advantage amongst the elderly."

YOUR CHALLENGE

What restores and energizes you?

How much do you read? Pick up a physical book and take a break from your screen.

Create a restorative morning ritual.

Invest in yourself, as I often do—including regular massages, reflexology, technology detox days, and maintaining boundaries—to protect valuable introverted 'me time.'

> *Our brains never get a break and the results can be increased stress, anxiety, insomnia and, if left unchecked, even depression But there is something you can do—nothing.*
>
> ~ Mathew Johnstone, author and cartoonist

SURROUND YOURSELF WITH NATURE

Nature gives you the face you have at twenty; it is up to you to merit the face you have at fifty.

~ Coco Chanel

Coco loved to be surrounded by flowers and to spend time walking amongst, or gazing upon, nature to replenish.

"I often found her alone sitting at her dressing table, gazing down into the garden, looking at the chestnut trees," recounts Claude Delay, now an imminent psychoanalyst who once knew Coco in her youth.

We all know the physical benefits of nature—being amongst plants and flowers boosts mental well-being. A series of published studies have shown clear links between gardening and positivity.

One study found levels of the stress hormone cortisol in those who gardened were considerably lower those who people who relaxed by reading.

Even the simple act of looking out a window to green space has been linked to reduced stress levels and faster recovery from illness.

"The garden brings stillness," says Lisa, a marketing executive who says she couldn't have survived her working life without a garden.

"Touching the soil is one of the most reenergizing things I can do. Everything slows down. My mind works differently. I don't set out to solve problems but the answers seem to come. These days if ever I am stressed it will be because I haven't been in the garden."

Similarly, Cathy who suffers from anxiety and depression finds solace in a small vegetable garden she started behind her flat.

"When I become immobilized by my anxiety, the garden gives me something achievable to get started on. Gardening is methodical I can go out there and think, 'What does my garden need?' It could be as simple as pulling caterpillars off some broccoli. Tuning in to this helps me get more in touch with things outside of myself."

YOUR CHALLENGE

Experience the healing power of nature. Whether you're blessed with green fingers or not, it doesn't matter what you doing—just that you get outside in some green space every day.

Monitor how much time you spend indoors. Schedule regular fresh air time.

> *Beauty surrounds us, but usually*
> *we need to be walking in a garden to know it.*
>
> ~ Rumi, Persian poet

WALK!

There is nothing more comfortable than a caterpillar and nothing more made for love than a butterfly.
We need dresses that crawl and dresses that fly. Fashion is at once a caterpillar and a butterfly—caterpillar by day, butterfly by night.

~ Coco Chanel

Coco Chanel spent much of her youth walking up and down the staircase, with its 36 stairs, leading from the orphanage to the The French Abbey of Aubazine—over and over again, from Vespers to Matins for over 7 years.

Did she sprint down the stairs—eager to get back to bed? Or did she walk slowly, her eyes down on the stairs, her head bowed in prayer?

Whether going to the Abby felt like a penance or a meditation Coco never said. But the emotional, mental and spiritual benefits for maintaining regular exercise, like walking, is well documented—boosting spirits, rejuvenating mental energy, and energizing the body.

When your breathing is calm and steady you are in a nurtured state, which also helps strengthen your immune system.

Researchers also confirm there is a strong link between breathing, outside energy and beneficial brainwave patterns.

Which may explain why so many people say that walking is their meditation—clearing their mind, and allowing space for good ideas to flourish.

YOUR CHALLENGE

Discipline yourself to go for a walk regularly—ideally outside and somewhere not too frenzied.

Oxygenate your mind and body—combine brisk walking with deep breathing to boost your energy levels, short-term memory, and state of mind.

Walking for me is my way of thinking, my way of meditating. It is not that I am thinking that I am in a kind of trance totally connected to the present moment.

~ Paulo Coelho, author

HEALTHY SPIRITUAL SIGNIFICANCE

Remember me, on earth or in heaven.

~ Coco Chanel

If we have unhealthy thoughts and feeling about our spiritual significance and life purpose, says Dr. Mona Lisa Schultz, a neuropsychiatrist and medical intuitive, we're more likely to have concerns with the following health problems: heart attack, stroke, cancer, or other life-threatening disease: a major automobile accident, fall or other serious mishap."

By rewiring your feelings and thoughts about your life's purpose and spiritual connection, you'll improve the health of your 'seventh' emotional centre—imbuing you with a sense of purpose in life, and a connection with the universe and a higher power.

To move toward health in the seventh emotional centre involves overcoming a lifelong emotional pattern of hopelessness and despair—something Coco Chanel battled to overcome throughout her life.

YOUR CHALLENGE

Feel as lovers do—unite with a higher power. Affirm your life purpose and sacred mission in life and feel more joyous.

Remind yourself of your life purpose, free yourself from grudges and resentments, and access a higher power.

To foster the ability to change in spite of your fears, use affirmations. For example, "I know I am worthwhile. It is safe for me to succeed. " Or, "I love and appreciate myself." Or some other empower affirmation to remind yourself that you are powerful, talented and worthy.

Compose your life in service to your God.

I was born out of due time in the sense that by temperament and talent I should have been more suited for the life of a small Bach, living in anonymity and composing regularly for an established service and for God.

~ Igor Stravinsky, composer

YOUR BODY BAROMETER

I am not young but I feel young. The day I feel old, I will go to bed and stay there. J'aime la vie!
I feel that to live is a wonderful thing.

~ Coco Chanel

Feeling tired, bored, sluggish—or simply exhausted? It's amazing how energy can be revived, and life prolonged, when you work with joy. Coco Chanel was still designing dresses and over-seeing her empire well into her eighties.

Doing things she loved kept her feeling young and well. She once said, "There is no time for cut-and-dried monotony. There is time for work. And time for love. That leaves no other time!"

When you don't do the things you love your health can suffer. Common signs of neglecting your passion can include, headaches, insomnia, tiredness, depression, anxiety, and irritability.

The body never lies, however, many people soldier on ignoring the obvious warning signs. It's easy to rationalize these feelings away, but the reality is your body is screaming out for something different.

YOUR CHALLENGE

When you feel unfulfilled or drained of energy what do you notice? How does this differ from times when you are passionate?

Work with passion—do something that inspires you. Even 15 minutes a day dedicated to passion will boost your energy.

Just as appetite comes from eating, so work brings inspiration, if inspiration is not discernible at the beginning.

~ Igor Stravinsky, composer

PRINCIPLE SEVEN: EMPOWER YOUR RELATIONSHIPS

MAINTAIN YOUR INDEPENDENCE

*I never wanted to weigh more heavily
on a man than a bird.*

~ Coco Chanel

Whether you work for yourself or with your life partner it's important to maintain your financial and personal independence.

Throughout history this is something that women have fought for and are still fighting for. Equality, reciprocity, and sharing—are all important elements of many successful relationships.

Weighing heavily on another person, waiting for a knight in gleaming armor to come and rescue you, or some other fictional notion of living a happily dependent life seldom achieves longevity. Even when the relationship endures, seeds of resentment can foster.

Coco Chanel learned a painful truth in childhood—she could not afford to rely on anyone. Certainly not her father—nor her lovers. Not in the long term.

Not if she was going to achieve the freedom she desired. Not to become the woman, the person, the success she believed was her destiny.

Boy Capel, the British playboy and industrialist betrayed her by marrying another woman, although their affair continued until his death in a car crash.

While she was devastated she wanted to be his equal. His rejection made her even more determined to maintain her financial independence, and the security that being able to fend for herself provided.

However independence taken too far can have its downsides. Sometimes being emotionally supported by another, and trusting others to care for you when you are in need, is a great comfort.

Interdependence in a relationship can enable you to have the best of both realms.

YOUR CHALLENGE

How can you maintain your independence?

What would you have to disbelieve about leaning on others that would support you?

*How a person masters his fate
is more important than what his fate is.*

~ Wilhelm von Humboldt, philosopher

LIVE WITH OTHERS

*One shouldn't live alone. It's a mistake.
I used to think I had to make my life on my own,
but I was wrong.*

~ Coco Chanel

While Coco was adept at getting powerful men to support her dreams she was less successful in securing an ever lasting commitment. She died aged 87. She was a rich successful woman—but alone.

She once said, A simple life, with a husband and children—a life with people you love—that is the real life." She also said, "Whatever her age, a woman needs to be looked after by a man who loves her... without that look she dies."

Only in her lonely old age did she realize that the truth that had eluded her. Perhaps if she had put as much energy into creating a successful intimate relationship as she did building her career she may have died a happier woman with no regrets.

YOUR CHALLENGE

How can you remain true to yourself while still surrounding yourself with those that love and support you?

Art is a lie that makes us realize truth.

~ Pablo Picasso, artist

FLEE FALSE LOVE

Jump out the window if you are the object of passion. Flee it if you feel it. Passion goes, boredom remains.

~ Coco Chanel

Much of Coco's love life was one of affairs. Perhaps she never felt she deserved a committed monogamous relationship with a man she loved.

Or perhaps the wounds of her past followed her like a shadow making her run from commitment, fearing abandonment.

Whatever her reasons, she knew false love can impede your success, rob your peace of mind, and break your heart

A great relationship is about two things:

1. Finding out the similarities

2. Respecting the differences

No respect, no love. It's hard to respect a married person who has affairs and lies to their spouse.

YOUR CHALLENGE

If the quality of your intimate relationships is causing you stress seek help to clarify the source. Work on your self-esteem if need be.

Love yourself more than your need to be in a dysfunctional relationship.

*Let the beauty we love
be what we do.*

~ Rumi, Persian mystic and poet

HEAL YOUR WOUNDS

I imposed black; it still going strong today, for black wipes out everything else around.

~ Coco Chanel

As very young children, we're literally 'psychic sponges' actively soaking up the images, emotions, and events in our environment.

If, as it was for Coco Chanel, your childhood was traumatic, the resulting irrational feelings and fears you are left with as adults are often buried deep in your subconscious.

Unless brought to the light for healing these buried wounds can exert a negative impact on your relationships, self-esteem and beliefs about the love you need, want and deserve.

Coco Chanel craved loved. She yearned to be accepted. She ached to realize the dream that sustained her in the Convent as she devoured illicitly obtained romance novels. Her deepest desire what that one day she would be the heroine of her own love story and be married happily ever after.

Tragically this never happened for her. Perhaps the wounds of her tainted impoverished past that she fought so hard to keep a secret, caught up with her. But what if low self-esteem and self-worth, prevented her from allowing others to see and love her true vulnerable self.

YOUR CHALLENGE

Bring to light the wounds of your past. Work with a skilled professional if necessary to bring healing.

Forgive those who have trespassed against you—including your parents. The chances are they have unresolved wounds too.

Nothing has a stronger influence psychologically on their environment and especially on their children than the unlived life of the parent.

~ Carl Jung, psychologist

LET THE CHILDREN PLAY

*As long as you know men are like children,
you know everything!*

~ Coco Chanel

Coco Chanel was the lover of many successful, powerful—and capricious men.

"Women have always been the strong ones of the world. The men are always seeking from women a little pillow to put their heads down on. They are always longing for the mother who held them as infants," she once said.

Her strategy for success was not to take their outbursts, or sudden and unpredictable changes in attitude or behavior seriously—instead she treated them playfully.

"Sometimes you have to suck it up," says Rachel the wife of a very successful, and sometimes highly stressed, chef. "I have to remind myself that it's not about me and just stay relaxed," she told me.

Men may be childish at times—but we love children don't we! What do children crave? Attention? Cuddles? To be your number one focus? To be left alone? Or just your unconditional love? We need the same things sometimes.

YOUR CHALLENGE

If you live with an alpha male, or someone with tempestuous moods, or a person with continual demands on your time or energy, consider how you may weather their emotional storms and seemingly incessant needs more playfully.

I know now that most people are so closely concerned with themselves that they are not aware of their own individuality, I can see myself, and it has helped me to say what I want to say in paint.

~ Georgia O'Keeffe, artist

CONFLICT HAPPENS

It's probably not just by chance that I'm alone. It would be very hard for a man to live with me, unless he's terribly strong. And if he's stronger than I, I'm the one who can't live with him.

~ Coco Chanel

While you need others to survive and thrive, success in work and in life is more likely when your relationships are harmonious.

But, as much as we all like to get on, sometimes conflict is inevitable. People may feel threatened by your success, they may deliberately try to thwart you, or they may misunderstand your motives and desires.

Your family and loved ones may resent the time you need to spend away from them. You may feel guilty for wanting more from your life.

You may clash with your business or intimate partners—as Coco did. People may try to rip you off, cheat you, rob you. Be prepared— conflict is inevitable, no matter how kind or good-hearted or savvy you feel you are.

As Coco said, 'I don't care what you think. I don't think about you at all.' Care more about how well you handle conflict when it happens, and plan your conflict-handling strategy appropriately.

YOUR CHALLENGE

What do others fear? How might this fear or anxiety bring 0ut the worst in them?

How might they want the best for you?

What are their agendas? How might they want the worst for you? Why might your success threaten them?

How sharp are your conflict resolution skills?

How are you unnecessarily or unknowingly creating conflict?

Learn from your experiences.

Perhaps others need to see, touch, feel, taste and smell your success before they can back you. Perhaps you do too! Succeed anyway!

I am a woman in process. I'm just trying like everybody else. I try to take every conflict, every experience, and learn from it. Life is never dull.

~ Oprah Winfrey, businesswoman

SHOW YOUR STRENGTH

Gentleness doesn't get work done unless you happen to be a hen laying eggs.

~ Coco Chanel

Having healthy boundaries in all of your relationships is key to being productive, healthy and happy. Very often having healthy boundaries requires assertiveness.

The challenge is that many people confuse being assertive with being aggressive. This often leads to passive behavior where people may feel like they aren't being heard, valued or respected.

Issues with boundaries also happen in other kinds of relationships. Another common example is a person who works from home and is constantly being interrupted by their family.

If they confuse being assertive with aggression then they may never ask their family to respect their time when they are working.

Whether you think being assertive is unpleasant or fear people won't like you if you show your strength, there'll come a time when you need to show some muscle.

So what exactly is the difference between being assertive and being aggressive? While the two may look similar from the outside, they are worlds apart.

1. Assertiveness comes from a place of valuing yourself as equal to others.

Rather than valuing yourself less than another person (passive) or valuing yourself more than another person (aggressive), assertiveness means you value yourself equal to others.

For example, in negotiations an assertive person knows that they are looking for a fair exchange of value on all sides. An aggressive person is more concerned with what they can get out of it and may use fear tactics to get it.

2. Assertiveness is done with the intention of hurting no one.

Because sometimes people react poorly to assertiveness, then it's easy to see why someone would confuse it with aggression. The truth is that when someone is being assertive they are doing so with the intention of hurting no one, including themselves.

Unfortunately, we can't control how other people react to our own assertiveness, so sometimes being assertive will lead to hurt feelings even if that was never the intention.

3. Assertiveness means you speak to the point.

An assertive person is not afraid to express their opinion and stand up for themselves, even if it won't be liked. In short, being assertive is done from a place of love for all (including oneself), whereas aggression comes from a place of fear.

Coco Chanel had to stand up for herself and her needs on many, many occasions in order to achieve a fair exchange of value. One of the most infamous examples was her ongoing battle with the brothers she went into partnership with to produce Chanel N°5.

She spent years in a protracted and often acrimonious and litigious negotiation to gain a fair share of the profits from the sales of Chanel N°5 from her business partners. Had she been gentle, the chances are she never would have won.

YOUR CHALLENGE

Be strong—speak up and fight to be respected if need be.

Take assertiveness classes if you find yourself passively accepting a less than fair deal.

Maintain your boundaries—push back when people breach them.

If I was a guy, they would think I'm just opinionated. But as a woman, I'm 'difficult.' I mean, I can't change sex

~ Dame Zaha Mohammad Hadid, architect

PRINCIPLE EIGHT: EMPOWER
YOUR WORK

BE A LOVE MARK

A life with people you love—that is the real life.

~ Coco Chanel

Conventional science teaches that the main role of the heart is to pump blood around your body. But that's just a tiny part of the heart's power.

Your heart has an intelligence far greater than your brain. Scientific studies also confirm that your heart has the biggest and most powerful electromagnetic field.

But the heart, like any major organ needs nourishment to perform miracles. Feed and oxygenate your heart with all the things and people you love.

True fervent love is not something you can turn on and off like a tap. It's an obsession so consuming it feeds your soul. It can be as tangible as a vocation, or a house or as intangible as a dream or an idea. You could be in love with anything.

Here's a few of the things Coco loved with a passion:

- Mysticism
- A cause
- Analyzing and understanding things
- Books
- Creativity
- The future
- Perfume
- An idea
- Freedom
- Independence
- Interesting and talented men

She created an enduring personal and professional brand through these love marks.

YOUR CHALLENGE

What captures your heart's interest and attention? List as many things as you can that you love passionately.

People feed off passions—not professions. Become a 'Love Mark' and magnetize people and opportunities toward you.

Maintain the balance—try 'the rocking chair test'…what would you regret never having achieved when you reach old age and reflect back on your life?

If there's no love, what then?

~ Leonardo da Vinci, artist

YOU MAY WANT to read more about how to be a love mark in my book Mid-Life Career Rescue: Employ Yourself —getBook.at/EmployYourself.

FOLLOW YOUR JOY

*There is no time for cut-and-dried monotony. There is time for work. And time for love.
That leaves no other time!*

~ Coco Chanel

"Ask a Leo about the secret of leadership or a successful life and they will invariably list passion and tenacity, and a predisposition towards joy as the proper tools for the job," writes Steven Weiss in his book, *Signs of Success: The Remarkable Power of Business Astrology*.

As a Leo, Coco exemplified this. She knew that you can succeed at almost anything if you follow your joy. This is where you soul meets the road, as a tyre meets the asphalt—accelerating you toward your preferred future and fueling your success.

When you tap into your joy, you tap into an unlimited reservoir of energy and enthusiasm.

The French take it further—of course! *Jouissance*, literally means orgasmic joy. It's derived from the word from *jouir* ("to enjoy"). Jouissance is to enjoy something a lot!

One of my favorite creativity experts Mihaly Czikszentmihaly refers to this as a state of "flow"

In a popular YouTube talk he asks, "What makes a life worth living? Money cannot make us happy." Instead, he urges us to learn from people who find pleasure and lasting satisfaction in activities that bring about this state of It's a state of transcendent"flow."

Coco Chanel was flowing when she designed her clothes, she was flowing when she attended to the minutest details of her garments (note re always have scissor and thread. For her, her work had a spiritual aspect —it wasn't a job, it was her vocation.

I feel like this when I write books like this. I love writing. I would willingly do this activity for free. This is a sign of flow, according to Mihaly Czikszentmihaly.

Others signs are the things that come easily or naturally to you—especially when combined with "*jouir*." I often refer to this state of flow as following your passion.

Some of the most common questions I'm asked by people who seeking coaching is,"How can I find out what I'm good at?" and "How can I be sure that I will enjoy it and succeed?"

Whilst these questions may seem daunting, the past is often a good predictor of the future. Often we just need reminding of the times and circumstances in our lives when we felt inspired or energized by something, the times when our skills just seemed to flow and the outcomes we achieved. Such times can provide clues to our passions and unique strengths and talents.

I feel most in flow when I am creating.

I also lose all track of time when I am painting. The most fulfilling part of this is creating something that is innately satisfying to me and that the recipient truly loves. I feel excited, energized and truly complete.

Sometimes before I sit down to paint I find it really hard to get going.

During such times I find Picasso's words of wisdom, "Inspiration has to find us working," motivates me into action.

I discipline myself and say I will give it 30 minutes and that's all. Very often I find that 3-4 hours later I am blissfully painting and find it hard to tear myself away. Writing posts and articles that help people to follow their bliss produces the same state. I feel a huge sense of purpose and people comment positively about my flow-inspired works.

I know Coco Chanel felt the same.

YOUR CHALLENGE

Find something you're passionate about and keep hugely interested in it, by feeding and nurturing your passion every day

Nothing you want is upstream. What comes easily you to you? What is a struggle?

Flow has to find you working—take action. Do what you love

Collect examples of people who followed their joy and made a rewarding career and/or enriched their lives

All My life I have been mistaken in measuring the significance of any work
by the struggles
that went into it.

~ Henri Matisse, artist

IF YOU NEED MORE help finding and living your life purpose you my book, Find Your Passion and Purpose: Four Easy Steps to Discover A Job You Want And Live the Life You Love, available as a audiobook, paperback and ebook from all good online stores.

DO THE WORK

My life didn't please me, so I created my life.

~ Coco Chanel

If there was one thing Coco Chanel wasn't afraid of it was hard work. Born into poverty she didn't have the luxury of procrastinating or deluding herself that someday, maybe tomorrow, she would do her greatest work.

It helped, of course, that she loved what she did with such a passion that work didn't feel like work at all.

But even when you love what you do, it can be a struggle to show up and do what you need to do. At times the tasks required to complete your finest work can lie outside your comfort or knowledge zone. Show up anyway.

You may be having a bad hair day. Show up anyway. Perhaps there's some drama on going around you, or you're just plain tired. Show up anyway—even if it's only for five or ten minutes or half an hour. Who knows, you may just find yourself re-inspired.

As Paulo Coelho, author of *The Alchemist*, shared on the Tim Ferris show, "I have the book inside me, I start procrastinating in the morning. I checked my emails, I check news—I check anything that I could check just to avoid the moment to sit and face myself as a writer in front of my book.

"For three hours I am trying to tell myself, 'No no no. Later later later.' Then later not to lose face in front of myself I tell myself to sit and write for half an hour, and of course, this half an hour becomes 10 hours in a row. That's why I write my books so quickly. Very quickly, because I cannot stop. *I cannot stop.* And then of course at night I take a lot of notes because I am still in the speed of writing the book, the next day these notes are useless.

The same thing happens again: checking emails, going to social communities, postponing, procrastinating. And this I cannot stop it's my ritual. I have to feel guilty of not writing for three hours or four hours. But then I start writing non-stop. In two weeks I have the book ready."

YOUR CHALLENGE

Surrender to procrastination—set a time limit and then get on with it!

Or, be a creative procrastinator—put off everything that doesn't advance your dreams

Show up! Show up! When you show up your muse will too! Just like mine did as I wrote this chapter—in five minutes, despite telling myself I would do it tomorrow—all thanks to James Patterson's quote below!

> *Do NOT sit there like 'Oh I don't feel like it today. I don't feel like it tomorrow'. Feel like it! Do it! Force yourself.*
>
> ~ James Patterson, author

TAKE YOUR CHANCE

A girl should be two things: who and what she wants.

~ Coco Chanel

In French *chance* means 'luck'. Chanel and Chance sound so similar as if they were created for each other.

Coco Chanel deeply believed in the power of luck—taking chances, and following opportunities defined her—even when there was no guarantee of success.

She believed in harnessing the arbiters of good fortune and the power of dreams and oracles as oracles of future success.

When she was a poor young woman cloistered in a convent orphanage she dreamed of a romantic life, fueling her dreams of happily-ever-after with romantic novels she read again and again.

When the chance came to live the life she had imagined she grabbed it —aligning herself with wealthy men who could provide the life she wanted.

So it's no surprise that one of her most popular and enduing perfumes is named '*Chance.*'

"Unexpected. Unpredictable. Irresistible. Delicately sparkling, endlessly romantic, vibrant, fresh and spirited," are just some of the words used to describe this popular perfume—it's no chance that they also define the woman behind the brand.

Upon Coco's death a pack of Tarot cards were discovered in her apartment, the number five, which was her lucky number, was on top. A collection of symbolic objects was scattered throughout her room. She looked for signs and symbols in the ordinary, a spray of roses, a pure white camellia, a Catholic icon, and also believed in theosophy. All of which boosted her belief in the power of chance and bolstered her confidence in taking inspiring action.

YOUR CHALLENGE

What irresistible idea or opportunity could you take a chance on?

What signs, symbols or spiritual practice could you harness to boost your confidence?

Success is defined by the things you say yes to—what makes you happy.

#Takeyourchance

Women are always told, 'You're not going to make it, it's too difficult, you can't do that, don't enter this competition, you'll never win it.' They need confidence in themselves and people around them to help them to get on.

~ Dame Zaha Mohammad Hadid, architect

BE ORIGINAL

*In order to be irreplaceable
one must always be different.*

~ Coco Chanel

Coco's commitment to reinventing herself in order to remain true to herself at any cost is the reason why, generation after generation, her name and her brand have persisted.

Chanel might have ended with the death in the 1970's of the complex woman who founded the businesses that carried her name, or have quietly disappeared from the cultural imagination.

Instead, both Coco Chanel and Chanel the business have proven astonishingly resilient. Originality, authenticity and reinvention was a crucial part of Chanel's success.

Your power to choose the focus of your life allows you to reinvent yourself, to change your future, and to powerfully influence the rest of your life—something Coco knew very well. "I invented my life by taking for granted that everything I did not like would have an opposite, which I would like," Coco once said. Coco also said, "Hard times arouse an instinctive desire for authenticity."

YOUR CHALLENGE

Whether you are bored, stressed, anxious or under economic attack, adapt to changing circumstances—reinvent your career and your life.

A big part of originality is following your own truth. If you think something is a great idea—try it. Don't get bogged down by fear or subscribing to other people's ideas and taking their work as your standard.

Be a trailblazer like all the great inventors, and have the satisfaction of being authentically you. Determine who you are and who you choose to be.

Create a life or work of heart that is as original as you are. Believe in your capacity for originality.

Take your opinion as your standard. Bring forth your passion and infuse your life and work with your true essence—all else will follow.

There will come a time when you believe everything is finished. That will be the beginning.

~ Louis L'Amour, novelist

KNOW WHEN TO CHANGE

*Don't spend time beating on a wall,
hoping to transform it into a door.*

~ Coco Chanel

To keep opportunities flowing you need to respond to the signs that it's time to open new doors. Your intuitive guidance, body barometer and willingness to reach beyond your current limitations, real or imagined, can be game-changer.

Living this way requires daring and playful leaps outside of your comfort zone, and moment-by-moment navigation. Even a small detour and following your curiosity can have a beneficial impact on your success.

Coco Chanel expertly blended intuitive instinct with an acute awareness of the forces that shaped demand for her products. The looming war guided her designs toward more practical, masculine lines and durable fabrics, women's cry for liberation from constraint inspired trousers and business suits, and the need to diversify her product range, motivated her to go in search of creating a perfume.

She was the consummate Renaissance woman—reinventing herself numerous times, she is one of the early adopters of what I call a "Career Combo"—threading different business activities throughout her career. Her ability to shape-shift enabled Coco to quickly adapt to changing fortunes.

For many successful people having several skills or jobs is the best way to manage unpredictable or unsustainable cash flow—and to finance a desired change of career.

For example, DJ lemon is passionate about music. However, his love for reggae music doesn't pay well, so he continues to combine his passion for music with working as a barber. Shelly is training to be a movie director, but knows she can fall back on her nursing skills when work is thin.

YOUR CHALLENGE

How can you tune into your instincts and heed the call for change?

What or who could support you to step outside of your comfort zone?

What new doors, or new world's would you like to break into? How will you feel when you have succeeded?

Do a career combo.

> *What the caterpillar calls the end of the world, the master calls the butterfly.*
>
> ~ Richard Bach, author

JEALOUS SABOTEURS

*I don't care what you think about me.
I don't think about you at all.*

~ Coco Chanel

Chanel's confidence, some say arrogance, was hard won. She'd worked her way up from literally nothing to become one of the most popular designers in the history of fashion. But with the coming of World War II, her fame would turn into infamy.

During the war, Chanel became mired in controversy. When the Nazis marched on Paris, Chanel responded by shutting down her business and becoming involved with Hans Gunther von Dincklage, a Nazi officer 13 years her junior. In return, von Dincklage allowed Chanel to continue to reside in her beloved Ritz Hotel.

Was Coco the Mata Hari of the fashion world?

Alternately the toast and scourge of Paris, Coco Chanel's reputation never fully recovered from her affair with this Nazi intelligence officer during World War II. But according to one historian, Chanel may have been more of a war hero than a war criminal.

Edmonde Charles-Roux, considered the most reliable of Chanel's biographers, has offered circumstantial but credible evidence that Chanel was sent by Walter Schellenberg, a ranking officer in German intelligence, on a peace mission to British prime minister Winston Churchill. Schellenberg was reportedly acting on behalf of Gestapo leader Heinrich Himmler, who attempted to offer secret peace initiatives to the Allies toward the end of the war.

Rumors surrounding this period abound. Coco is lucky she escaped with her life. Other weren't so lucky. Mata Hari, an exotic dancer and high class courtesan, seven years Coco's senior, was executed in her 40's for similar 'crimes'—loving men regardless of nationality, and as a result being accused of treason. Chanel called in favors from the powerful men in her life—favors Mata Hari also tried to call to no avail.

After the liberation of France, French resistance forces arrested Chanel for her wartime activities. But Churchill, a close friend of one of Chanel's former lovers, the Duke of Westminster, is said to have intervened on her behalf. Chanel was released just 24 hours after her arrest and immediately left France for Switzerland.

Was Coco a spy? I doubt it. Was she a survivor? Undoubtedly. And does any of it all really matter now? Westerners are now bedfellows of the Russians, Chinese, Japanese, Germans—all those people we fought and died for—men and women with hearts and dreams and a wish for peace, just as she did.

YOUR CHALLENGE

Others may be jealous or critical of your success—succeed anyway!

Wage war on your enemy. Shoot down your saboteurs with your nonchalance.

I had another dream the other day about music critics. They were small and rodent-like with padlocked ears, as if they had stepped out of a painting by Goya.

~ Igor Stravinsky, composer

GIVE GENEROUSLY

Hard times arouse an instinctive desire for authenticity.

~ Coco Chanel

It's a myth that only the mean and cruel amass success. Born in a poor house, and raised in a convent founded by the saintly Étienne, a man renown for his gifts of charity, Coco Chanel experienced first hand the blessings of those who gave generously to those in need.

Throughout her life she returned these blessings to others, including financially supporting the struggling composer Igor Stravinsky, impoverished exiled Tzars, and fallen Russian aristocracy to whom she gave employment.

Raised by The Church she would have been familiar with St Nicholas and legendary generosity which led him to be called 'Santa Claus' and become a patron saint of children and the needy. One of the most famous stories about him describes his rescue of three young girls whose father was about to send them into prostitution to save the impoverished family.

The saint threw three bags of gold through the girls' bedroom window so that their future was secure.

When you contribute with joy and give to others from the spirit of love, and are totally detached from the outcome of your offering, you'll be surprised at how the Universe gives back to you

YOUR CHALLENGE

The more you give, the more your receive. Start or continue giving time, money, assistance, or goods to those in need. This will help affirm how much you have, and lead to larger feelings of abundance—which in turn automatically attract greater prosperity into your life.

Call upon St Nicholas to inspire and guide your volunteer work and show you the best avenues to give donations.

Keep a gratitude journal and give thanks daily for everything you are grateful for. List some ways you could pay your good fortune forward —it may be as simple as telling someone how much you appreciate them.

There is some strange alchemy associated with gratitude. Somewhere along the way of doing these lists, I fell in love with my life again.

~ Anne Dowsett Johnston, author and recovering alcoholic

CONCLUSION

CONCLUSION: BEAUTY AND THE BEST

"The heavens often rained down the richest gifts on human beings, naturally, but sometimes with lavish abundance bestow upon a single individual beauty, grace and ability, so that, whatever he does, every action is so divine that he distances all other men, and clearly displays how his genius is the gift of God and not a requirement of human art."

~ Giorgio Vasari, *Lives of The Artists*

The belief in power of beauty was central to everything Coco Chanel pursued. Inspired by astrology, tarot, numerology, theosophy and the divine healing power of the plant world, she knew that nature and spirituality held the immortal secrets of both beauty and power.

"Fashion has two purposes: comfort and love. Beauty comes when fashion succeeds," she once said.

While Coco is arguably most famous as a designer, she was the archetype of a Renaissance woman, whose unquenchable zest for life was equalled only by the power of her determination, vision and aptitude for creation.

Beauty is timeless, holding sacred universal wisdom and truth. The artist Paul Klee once said, 'One eye sees and the other feels'. And it is this ability to touch our souls is where Coco Chanel has surpassed many others.

BEAUTY AND YOUR SUCCESS

Beauty comes from the inside. It's your essence—so authentic that, just as there will never be another Coco, there will never be another you.

The art of success lies in bringing more beauty into this world. It lies in being you. It's a secret that ancient masters and philosophers understood well. And it's a secret that modern day successful people also know and harness.

Businessmen and women, politicians, and the most successful artists understand that intrinsic, authentic, soulful beauty attracts. Beauty is irresistible. Beauty sells.

You may not be aiming to create the next acclaimed perfume, but if you infuse your life and your work with your energy, power, talent and essence, who knows—100 years from today somebody may well be writing a book about you and the legacy you left.

You may think the outcome has to happen in a certain way, on a certain day, to reach your goal. But human willpower cannot make everything happen. Spirit has its own idea, of how the arrow flies, and upon what wind it travels.

It may not happen overnight, but if you follow your heart, maintain your focus, and take inspired action your time will come.

I promise!

If due to some strange twist of fate, it doesn't? At least you'll know you tried. A life of no regrets—now that's worth striving for.

Let the beauty you love be the life that you live. Now go out and create great art!

THE TRUTH ABOUT SUCCESS

Everyday is a fashion show and the world is the runway.

~ Coco Chanel

I've distilled Coco's principles for success down to twenty-one facts... or TRUTHS as I call them. And the wonderful thing is that these truths can be embodied by you. You can be, have and do whatever your heart desires if you're determined to succeed and look for ways to put these truths into practice.

1 Love

2 Talent

#3 Curiosity

#4 Learning

#5 Interest

#6 Vision

7 Service/Purpose

\# 8 Opportunity

#9 Focus

#10 Commitment

#11 Values

#12 Motivation

#13 Labor

#14 Asking

#15 Goals

#16 Optimism

#17 Virtue/Integrity

#I18 Instinct

#19 Strength

#20 Energy

#21 Determination

I KNOW you can succeed at whatever you set your heart, mind and soul to. Pursue your liberty—be free to be you. Have the courage and confidence to define success on your own terms.

Follow your passions, cultivate your natural and dormant talents, remain curious and embrace learning, follow your interests, maintain your vision, work with purpose and be of service.

When opportunity knocks, open the door. If it doesn't knock, go out and create opportunities. Focus on what you desire, not what you fear. Commit—devote yourself to your quest for success.

Let your values guide you—they are your truth-compass. Clarify what motivates you, be this extrinsic or intrinsic rewards. Do the work—no matter how small the effort, in time you will amass success.

Ask your way to success, and learn from those with the skill, knowledge and power to help you. Don't be shy, proud or nervous to ask for help!

Set goals—little, bigger and bigger still. Stretch and grow and strive to make the impossible possible. Celebrate your successes along the way—no matter how small.

Cultivate optimism—water it regularly and never let faith and hope wither from neglect.

Maintain your integrity and virtue. Follow your hunches, intuition and instinct. Be grateful for all that you have—be it health, friends, support, or your cat.

Maximize your energy—look after your mind, body and soul. And lastly, but perhaps also firstly, play.

Alleviate the pressure—don't take yourself too seriously. Be joyful in success—and also while attempting success. Keep your feet on the ground, your head in the clouds and ride the magic carpet of your creative imagination.

But most of all, 'do a Coco'—stand out from the crowd and dare to be different, even if others think you're crazy!

> *It's better to be absolutely ridiculous than absolutely boring.*
>
> ~ Marilyn Monroe, actress

The two men I've loved, I think, will remember me, on earth or in heaven, because men always remember a woman who caused them concern and uneasiness. I've done my best, in regard to people and to life, without precepts, but with a taste for justice.

~ Coco Chanel

SUMMARY OF HOLISTIC STRATEGIES

Throughout this book you've discovered ways to overcome anxiety, build resilience and find joy by increasing your ability to cope. Regular exercise, good diet, relaxation exercises, and rest are a few of the many techniques we've covered.

Listed below are some helpful reminders of some of the many holistic coping strategies we've explored or touched on that you can call upon during times of current or anticipated need. Some of those listed below will be covered in other books in the *Anxiety Rescue* series.

Physical

- Learn to listen to your body
- Adequate exercise
- Getting outside
- Physical touch/massage
- Muscle relaxation
- Sleep
- Warmth

- Relaxation breathing
- A healthy diet, i.e. reducing stimulants (coffee, nicotine, sugar etc.), increasing water, and eating organic non-processed foods, watching for allergies
- Yoga
- Tapping

Behavioral

- Balanced lifestyle
- Support groups / Counseling
- Sharing with friends and family
- Humor
- New interests / activities
- Hobbies
- Socializing
- Entertaining
- Taking time out
- Music / dancing / singing/creative expression
- Meditating
- Yoga
- Being proactive and taking control of the situation
- Change careers
- Reducing or eliminating alcohol consumption
- Making time to do nothing at all

Cognitive / Perceptual (thinking)

- Rational thinking techniques to help change the way you interpret the stressful situation

- Positive thinking/cultivating optimism
- Self-assertion training
- Personal development
- Building self-esteem
- Realistic goal planning
- Time management
- Learning to say "No"
- Priority clarification
- Reflection
- Mindfulness
- Acceptance
- Hypnosis

EMOTIONAL

- Releasing emotions and expressing feelings (laugh, talk, cry, write in a journal, paint etc.)
- Learning how to "switch off"
- Taking time out
- Solitude and space
- Intimacy
- Counseling and support
- Challenging your emotional reactions to situations
- Passion/Joy

Social

- Scheduling time to spend with important people in your life
- Making plans with friends, family and loved ones in advance
- Sharing your experiences of stress with certain people in your

life, especially letting them know the ways that stress has been affecting you, so they understand
- Practicing assertive communication within your significant relationships to decrease conflicts, while also continuing to find ways to show people around you that they are important

Spiritual

- Prayer and mediation—scheduling regular time
- Helping others (talking, writing, supporting)
- Reiki and other energy healing techniques
- Talking with a spiritual confidant or leader to explain any spiritual issues or doubts that you may have encountered
- Forgiveness (of self or others)
- Compassion / loving kindness
- Continuing to read and learn about your faith, belief or value system
- Connecting with others who share your beliefs

Is your job making you anxious? Read the following FREE excerpt from my popular *Mid-Life Career Rescue Series: Employ Yourself*. Learn how to break the cycle of anxiety and depression by becoming your own boss.

EXCERPT: MID-LIFE CAREER RESCUE (EMPLOY YOURSELF)

CHOOSE AND GROW YOUR OWN BUSINESS WITH CONFIDENCE

You don't always need buckets of money, or the courage of a lion, to start your own business. Plenty of successful entrepreneurs have started their businesses on a shoe-string budget and launched new careers while combining salaried employment. Many have felt the fear and launched their business anyway.

I was in my mid-30's, a single parent, holding down a steady job, when I started my first business, Worklife Solutions. I was worried and fearful that I'd fail, but I did it anyway. It's one of the most creative, joyful endeavors I've ever done.

Since then I've created many more businesses and helped people all over the globe become successfully self-employed. Like some of the people who share their stories in this book, and other budding entrepreneurs who've taken a strategic route to finance their businesses.

When I first started out in business over a decade ago, I thought about all the people I knew, or had read about, that were successful in their own business. What I found then, still applies today. The list below is what they have in common. As you read this list think how many strategies could apply to you:

They were doing something they love; their passion drove them.

Making money was not their sole motivation. Their businesses grew from a desire to serve others; they were not trying to force something on others or to make a killer sale. Instead, they wanted to make a positive difference and create something of value. They didn't badger people into buying their goods or service.

1. **They cared about whether or not they could help a prospective client.** If they could, great. If not, they were either quietly persistent until they were needed, or they moved on.
2. **They planned for success.** Their business and marketing plans were living documents and they managed their finances extraordinarily well.
3. **They shared.** They communicated their vision, goals and plans with those important to them, and they researched their clients and stakeholders constantly to learn how to do things better *together*.
4. **They listened.** They listened to their staff, their families and their clients. Then, and only then, when they understood their issues, fears, needs and desires did they offer a solution.
5. **They started smart.** When employing others, whether on contract or as salaried staff, they hired the right people for the right job, and employed people who were strong in areas they were not. When skill gaps appeared, they gave their people

the training, systems, environment and recognition to do their job well.
6. **They took calculated risks.** They always looked before they leapt, but they leapt nonetheless. Courage and confidence was something they built as they went.
7. **They believed in themselves, or faked it!** Even professionals doubt themselves—but they don't let self-doubt win.

"YOU HAVE to believe in yourself. Even when you don't, you have to try," encourages Serena Williams, tennis super-star and 23-time Grand Slam champion.

"There are moments when I am on the court and I'm like, 'I don't think I'm going to be able to do this'. But then I fortify myself and say, 'I can, I can'–and it happens. If you believe in yourself, even if other people don't, that really permeates through and it shows. And people respect that."

IF THE STRATEGIES above sound like things you can do, or are willing to try, chances are self-employment is right for you. But to double check, try the following Entrepreneurial Personality Quiz.

THE ENTREPRENEURIAL PERSONALITY QUIZ

Do you have the right personality to be an entrepreneur? Are you better suited to becoming a Franchisee? Would contracting suit you better? Or is paid employment really the best option after all?

Before committing yourself to starting your own business of any type, you need to ask yourself whether you have what it takes.

The following quiz is written as though you are still in a salaried role. If you have already started your own business, respond to the questions as though you are still in your last job. Answer as you really are, not how you would like to be.

1. Is accomplishing something meaningful with your life important to you?
2. Do you typically set both short and long-term goals for yourself?
3. Do you usually achieve your goals?
4. Do you enjoy working on your own?
5. Do you like to perform a variety of tasks in your job?
6. Are you self-disciplined?
7. Do you like to be in control of your working environment?

THE ENTREPRENEURIAL PERSONALITY QUIZ

8. Do you take full responsibility for your successes and failures?
9. Are you in excellent physical, mental, and emotional health?
10. Do you have the drive and energy to achieve your goals?
11. Do you have work experience in the type of business you wish to start?
12. Have you ever been so engrossed in your work that time passed unnoticed?
13. Do you consider 'failures' as opportunities to learn and grow?
14. Can you hold to your ideas and goals even when others disagree with you?
15. Are you willing to take moderate risks to achieve your goals?
16. Can you afford to lose the money you invest in your business?
17. When the need arises, are you willing to do a job that may not interest you?
18. Are you willing to work hard to acquire new skills?
19. Do you usually stick with a project until it is completed?
20. Does your family support and stand by you in everything you do?
21. Are you organized and methodical in your work?
22. Does it frustrate you when you can't buy the things you want?
23. Do you like taking calculated gambles?
24. Would you still want your own business, even if there were plenty of other good jobs?
25. Are you a people person?
26. Do you handle personal finances well?
27. As an employee did you/do you regularly suggest new ideas at various levels?
28. Do you feel that you can truly shape your own destiny?
29. How flexible are you when approaching work tasks? If things become difficult do you adapt and complete the task?
30. Is the money you could make one of the primary reasons for starting your own business?

Scoring:

Your answers to at least 20 of these questions should be yes if you are to be successful as a business owner.

THE ENTREPRENEURIAL PERSONALITY QUIZ

The more 'yes' answers, the more likely you are to enjoy the entrepreneurial life and be successful as a business owner.

It is not necessary to answer yes to each of these questions, but if you answer no to some of them you will want to evaluate what that means to you and how significantly it may impact your ability to run your own business.

SUCCESS STORY: A FORK IN THE ROAD

Sheree Clark followed her enthusiasm—her passion for helping others and sharing what she had learned through her own life challenges led her to start her coaching business.

The seeds of change were also cultivated during a stressful time in her life and her former job. She shares her journey of mid-life career reinvention below:

> "My current business is Fork in the Road. I am a healthy living (life) coach. I chose the name initially because I was focused on food and healthful eating, and since "fork" conjures up the idea of eating, it seemed to fit. I also believe that at any given point we are all at a proverbial fork in the road.
>
> That fork can be a major one—such as a career choice or the decision to enter or leave a marriage—or a small one, like whether to say yes to dessert or being on another committee. So, when the focus of my business shifted to life coaching for women over 40, the name was still (and perhaps even more) fitting for my practice.

SUCCESS STORY: A FORK IN THE ROAD

Fork in the Road is truly a crescendo of all of my life experience. I work with my clients to transform their health, reclaim vitality and mental focus, and help ensure they gain clarity on their vision and purpose. These are all things I have done for myself over the course of the last 6+ decades of life.

Deciding what to do

My first business was a marketing communications (advertising) agency that I was "talked into" co-founding in 1985 by a (then) new boyfriend. The truth is, I had grown bored at my job at a local university and had even announced my resignation, effective the following academic year (long notices are an accepted practice at US academic institutions). In the meantime, I had met—and fallen in love with—my later-to-be business partner, and the rest fell into place.

He convinced me that my skill set as a teacher, advisor and mentor would transfer easily to the business development aspect of running an advertising agency. We stayed business partners for 25 years (although the romantic aspect tanked after the initial 14 years).

My current business began after I decided to leave the agency world and (my now-ex) behind.

During my time owning the agency, I had taken a variety of classes simply out of an interest in personal development. Many of the courses had to do with health, nutrition and emotional maturity.

Eventually, as I became less interested in the marketing work and more involved in the business of human potential, it became harder to rally enthusiasm for owning an agency.

Finally, just as we were preparing to commemorate 25 years in business together, I told my partner I wanted to exit our partnership to begin something new.

SUCCESS STORY: A FORK IN THE ROAD

At that point, I still wasn't certain what my new work would look like, but I knew it wasn't fair to anyone (most especially me!) to stay where I knew I was no longer fully engaged.

So, in essence, I quit—and then I figured it out.

Finding an idea that would be successful—ask your way to success

I found the right product for the right market by trial and error! Next to creating a vision board, the informational interview is my favorite tool for helping me get back on track when I'm feeling lost.

When I was feeling unfulfilled in my business I scheduled a series of interviews with fellow entrepreneurs. I picked women who owned businesses. The only thing they had in common was that I really respected them, even though some I had never met in person.

One of my interviews was with the publisher of a local business newspaper: a fabulous lady who is probably 20 years my senior. We had our meeting over lunch and I told her, candidly, about my inner feelings. I told her I was hoping she might shed some light.

I asked her what she thought my skill sets and offerings were and where I might be able to plug the gaps. Her feedback? She said she had always thought of me as a teacher and a coach. She said she saw me as articulate, smart and capable, (which in itself is nice to hear, especially coming from someone you admire).

And then she offered up a casual suggestion. She said, "You've always had a way with words. Why don't you write a column for a publication in your industry or some area of your life that brings you joy." Well, that was an idea that resonated, and if nothing else was worth seeing if I could make happen.

SUCCESS STORY: A FORK IN THE ROAD

The payoff

I went back to my office and sent a query letter to the editor of a graphic design magazine I had written for once or twice before, and asked if they were looking for writers.

Within an hour my phone rang. It was the editor himself. His words nearly knocked me off my chair. He said, "Wow, what timing! We are starting a business advice column in the next quarter, wanna write it?"

I ended up writing that column for five years. Not only did it help scratch an itch I was feeling, I made some extra money in the process. Now, I am not saying you'll have such epic results. But I do know that I have never had an informational interview without a payoff, even if it was just that I got to know somebody a little better.

Working your offerings into your own area of genius

It's not just about finding the right products and services, it's also about working your offerings into your own area of genius.

At this point in my life, while I enjoy making a good income, it's not only about maximizing revenue. I want to do work that brings me joy. I want to work with clients who are a fit for me, so that when I look at my calendar/schedule, I feel excitement, rather than dread.

In my instance, I am what we call a "Baby Boomer" (defined in the USA as being those born between 1946 and 1965). My generation and those slightly after, are all experiencing some major life challenges right now. Our jobs are changing or we've been laid off or deemed "redundant."

Our marriages and family structures are shifting or crumbling: we may suddenly become caretakers or divorcees or widows. Hell, our own bodies are changing and often it feels as though they are betraying us. And for many women over 40, after putting the needs of others first for much of our lives, we can finally say, "it's MY turn now."

What I just described is my area of genius. It's the arena I do best in and it's where I feel most at home. Having for the most part successfully navigated the challenges of being a 40, 50, 60-year old, I get to share my secrets and techniques with other women.

Starting fresh—financing a new career

In both cases when I started my companies I left what I had been doing to embark on the new thing. In the first instance (co-founding the agency) I felt safe doing so because I had a partner and so my risk/exposure was shared.

In the second instance (becoming a coach), I had the luxury of having built savings from the first endeavor, so I could plunge into the second. I recognize that not everyone will have such good fortune.

In both cases, I didn't need any start-up capital.

If I were to give advice, I'd say that while of course you have to consider your own financial situation, also take stock of your risk tolerance.

Entrepreneurship is not certain. There are all sorts of risks and no guarantees. If a lack of financial uncertainty makes you nervous, it's certainly safer to ease into being a business owner, but it can also be more challenging. There are only so many hours in a day!

Finding the confidence to leave the security of a regular salary

It wasn't confidence that propelled me into my second business. It was the pain of not living authentically.

SUCCESS STORY: A FORK IN THE ROAD

It would be an understatement to say that to close the ad agency I had co-founded was not a decision my former partner and I made easily or lightly. For almost half our lives we had been partners and close friends. But the time had come and we each wanted to do other things with our lives.

I had found a passion in the health and nutrition arena after receiving my certifications as a raw vegan chef and nutrition counselor.

My business partner discovered a love of fine art, and a desire to work more independently. Quite frankly, we both had become rather miserable in our roles as principals and we each needed new challenges.

Despite my excitement for my new future I struggled to dismantle what we had so carefully created. At the time, we decided to close the agency, it was still healthy but my partner's and my passions were on life support.

There were many signs that it was time for a change. I started to dread the out of town travel for clients that I had once so loved. He began to come into the office later and leave earlier.

We both had less patience for employee mistakes and client indecision. For me the defining moment came on a Sunday at church when I actually cried not because the sermon was so moving, but because I knew that in less than 24 hours I had to "go back to work."

It was clearly time to do something.

There are those who have applauded both of us for having the courage to do something so drastic, and others who deem us insane when we could be 'so close to retirement.' All I know is that, as scary as it was, it has rekindled the adrenalin rushes I have not felt in a very, very long time. It was absolutely the right thing to do.

Finding customers

My clients typically follow me online for a period of time before contracting with me for services. Often they run across me because I am a guest speaker at live events, or a subject matter expert on television, or a guest on an online interview series or summit. Others may have been referred to me by a friend or a colleague.

The marketing activities which have been most important and successful for me are speaking and interviews. I also write guest blogs and articles.

Maintaining balance

Running a business should not be a 24/7 thing! Although there are absolutely "push" times, especially in the beginning, I think down time and rest are essential to business success

Down time, time to refuel, is made possible by setting priorities, delegation and hiring (or subcontracting) efficiently. I personally find balance by planning my days the night before.

Each night before I go to bed, I establish what the most important project or priority is for the next day, and that project is the first thing I address after I do my exercise and meditation.

I also find that sometimes I have to actually schedule in my fun times. With my current work schedule, I coach clients the first three weeks of the month.

The last week of every month I take off from individual coaching, and that is when I attend to personal matters such as doing errands, scheduling salon services and meeting friends for social engagements.

I still do work during that fourth week, but because I don't typically schedule client appointments, I have time for other things.

Keeping energy levels high

It's not hard to have high energy when you have high enthusiasm. I love what I do and it keeps me young, vital, engaged and energized. That said, taking care of yourself mentally emotionally and spiritually is also critical. I get adequate sleep, exercise and nutrition. I spend time in nature and in contemplation or prayer.

I have deep relationships. AND I have a coach. That may sound odd, because I AM a coach, but I believe those of us who are most successful, have gotten where we're at with help in identifying blocks, challenges and opportunities. That is what a coach does!

The secret to success, managing cash flow, and generating regular income

For me personally, I have always benefitted from finding and utilizing a good business coach and what is often called a 'mastermind community.' A mastermind is a group of like-minded people who meet regularly to share strategies and tackle challenges and problems together. They lean on each other, give advice, share connections and do business with each other when appropriate.

It's very much peer-to-peer mentoring, and it works! In terms of managing cash flow: one piece of advice is to not take your foot off the 'new business development' gas pedal when you get busy with other things. What you do today will determine your level of success tomorrow.

The learning curve

The biggest learning curve I had was going from owning a company that sold its services in a business to business arena (the communications agency) to one that provided services via a business to consumer model (my coaching practice).

SUCCESS STORY: A FORK IN THE ROAD

These two ways of conducting business are drastically different. Again, by seeking guidance from peers and by hiring a coach I was able to manage the amount of growing pain.

The best times in my business have usually been the "firsts." First client, first employee, first million-dollar year. The worst have usually been the result of going against my own intuition. Hiring someone I had a gut feeling about because they looked good on paper. Taking a poorly calculated risk because I was listening to my ego instead of looking at the facts or my intuition.

One of the best business books I have read is, *Turning Pro* by Steven Pressfield. It applies to everyone, but entrepreneurs especially.

What advice would you give to someone who has never started a business or been self-employed?

Start by taking the time to meet with other entrepreneurs and ask them a few questions about things that may have you concerned or sparked your curiosity.

This book, *Mid-Life Career Rescue: Employ Yourself*, is a great start, because it gives you a general 'peek under the tent' at being a business owner, but I would also speak to others in real time.

I often urge my clients to schedule what I refer as an 'informational interview' when they are considering going down new paths or are feeling stuck in some area of their lives.

What are the steps to self-employment? Is there a "right" order?

I have taken the leap to self-employment twice, and each time was different from the other. I think there are too many factors to make a generalized bit of advice valuable here. One caveat I would say to the analytical readers is "don't overthink it."

SUCCESS STORY: A FORK IN THE ROAD

With my current business, I began by sending a letter to everyone I knew from my former business, telling them what I was transitioning to, and straight-out asking them if they might be interested in my services, or if they would be willing to make a referral. I had enough takers to be encouraged to keep going!

Making the leap sooner

I would have left my first company to start my second company sooner. I was afraid of letting people down: my former partner, my employees, my clients. By the time I left, my passion was on life support.

If I could offer one piece of advice related to starting your own business and employing yourself it would be to know that being an entrepreneur can be lonely sometimes. Your friends, the ones who are employed by others, will think you have it made now.

They will believe that you have all the time in the world to do what you want, and that you're rolling in the money. They'll think you can go on lavish vacations and that you don't have to answer to anyone. Take heart: The other business owners you meet will know the real story.

The secret to self-employed success

Passion. Without it you may be mildly successful, but you'll never be wildly successful!"

Find out more about Sheree's passion-driven business here—www.-fork-road.com. Listen to our interviews here http://www.cassandragaisford.com/media and http://www.cassandragaisford.com/podcast/

I loved, loved, loved what Sheree shared and devoured every word—best of all there were no calories…so that was marvelous. What resonated with you?

SUCCESS STORY: A FORK IN THE ROAD

Identify and record any lessons can you learn from Sheree's experience of discovering her calling and setting up her business which you could apply to starting your own business. Summarize some possible action steps.

WHAT YOU'VE LEARNED SO FAR

- Before committing yourself to starting your own business or being self-employed, you need to ask yourself whether you have what it takes
- Follow your heart, let your passion and intuition guide you towards the business you were born to create
- You have to believe in yourself—even when you don't
- You don't always need buckets of money, or the courage of a lion, to start your own business. You can start on a shoestring and feel the fear and begin anyway

- Starting a business doesn't have to be a full-time gig. You can start small and keep your current job while you watch your baby grow
- Caring about people and delivering something of value is the key to success

What's Next?

So, now you know the pitfalls of being self-employed and you know some of the joys. But do you really understand what YOU are looking for and why?

The next chapter will help you clarify the motivating forces driving your decisions. Knowing these will help boost your confidence when it comes to making an inspired leap.

WHY DO YOU WANT TO BE YOUR OWN BOSS?

*"Wild horses wouldn't drag me back
to working for someone else."*
Alan Sugar, Entrepreneur and host of The Apprentice, UK

So now you know the pitfalls of being self-employed and you know some of the joys. But do you really understand what YOU are looking for and why?

Perhaps you can identify with Laura who wants to balance work commitments with caring for her young son. "My boss insists I go to the office. I can't understand why he won't let me work from home."

Do Your Own Thing

Creating your own business is one of the few ways you can generate an income doing what you want, when you want, with whom you want.

It can also be a great way to create an asset—one you can grow and sell later for a profit if you plan things right.

Employing yourself is also a great way to get a job when nobody else will hire you, or when you've lost your job. Like Wendy Pye (her story is shared below), who started her own company and went from redundant to becoming a multi-millionaire.

Running your own business doesn't mean that you are going to be chained to your desk 24/ 7 as some people mistakenly believe. One of the important things prior to starting any new venture is to determine what you want to achieve and why.

ACTION TASK! **Clarify what you really want**

Write a list of benefits that self-employment will offer you. If you run out of ideas the following list may help. Identify how you want to feel, and what you want to have, and why this is important to you.

BENEFITS OF SELF **Employment**

Listed below are some of the benefits many people gain from being self-employed. Make a note of those most relevant to you and add these to the list you generated above.

Assess any options you are considering by creating a decision-making criteria checklist. For example, if time freedom is important for you,

you may want to reconsider any plans to open a business where people expect you to be there at fixed hours.

- Time freedom—hours to suit yourself
- Flexibility
- No forced retirement age
- Autonomy
- Independence
- Making your own decisions
- Creativity
- Control
- Security–not worrying about corporate layoffs
- Live and work anywhere in the world
- Work from home
- Accountability
- Higher earnings
- Satisfaction and personal fulfillment
- Variety and freedom to be able to work on new ideas and create your own authentic style
- Combine diverse areas of interest, skill and enthusiasm
- Being guided by what feels right in your heart and intuition
- Freedom from financial stress
- Making a difference
- Freedom from the daily grind—a business that runs without you
- Being able to put all your passion and energy into something you believe in, rather than something someone else believes in
- Creating an income producing asset

From Redundant to Multi-Millionaire

Necessity, as some say, is the mother of invention–and often it is the extra push many people need to take a leap into something new.

Some 55,000 New Zealanders are so-called 'necessity entrepreneurs,' people prompted by redundancy or unemployment to set up their own businesses, as distinct from 'opportunity entrepreneurs,' who've become self-employed as a result of planning and choice.

Wendy Pye is the mother of all necessity entrepreneurs. It took a good dose of adversity to get her entrepreneurial juices flowing and she hasn't looked back. She was dumped without warning from NZ News after 22 years with the company, given five minutes to clear her desk, and then marched off the premises.

With no job to go to Pye, then aged 42, set up her own educational publishing company. Now a multi-millionaire, she admits her motivation for going it alone was a desire to show her former employers what she could do.

"I was devastated and disappointed. But it really changed my life, which is a lot better now than if [redundancy] had never happened. I needed the push."

She certainly showed her former employers just what she could do. The 2015 National Business Review's Rich List, estimates Pye's personal wealth at $105 million.

She has fond thoughts for that executive who laid her off all those years ago. "That guy had vision," she says. "He knew something I didn't know. I can say that and laugh now."

Dubbed one of New Zealand's women powerbrokers, Dame Wendy recently won the Business Entrepreneur category in the Women of Influence Awards.

The passion, determination and drive that helped her build her business into one of the most successful education export companies in the world shows no sign of slowing as she heads into her 70s.

Wendy Pye Publishing can now celebrate more than 2000 titles, in more than 20 countries, which have sold over 218 million copies. Her business has also developed digital learning platforms designed to teach children to read and write.

EXCERPT: MID-LIFE CAREER RESCUE (EMPLOY YOURSELF)

. . .

Age is On Your Side

Age is no barrier to employing yourself. Growing numbers of 40-plus men and women are taking up new challenges and starting businesses everyday. Being your own boss gives you more control over your future. If you love what you're doing, chances are you'll never want to retire.

Your life expectancy is on the rise. Which also means you'll be wanting enough money to live comfortably. Employing yourself will help you achieve that.

Ready to learn some new tricks?

As Brian Jones writes in his wonderful book, *Over 50? Start Your Business: Build Wealth, Control Your Destiny. Leave a Legacy*: "Within the last twenty years, technologies such as functional magnetic response imaging (FMRI) have debunked the old-dog-new-tricks myth. Scientists have found that the brain can grow and make new connections at any age. The scientific term for this is neuroplasticity.

Now more than ever you can be, do and have nearly anything you desire. Like Annie, who aged 54, left teaching and became a romance writer.

Compelling Evidence of Mid-Life Success

Loads of people have employed themselves or started their businesses in mid-life and beyond. Here's just a few:

- Joseph Campbell started Campbell's soup at age 52
- Arianna Huffington started the Huffington post at age 54
- Estee Lauder founded her cosmetics empire when she was 54
- Charles Flint started IBM at 61

- Amadeo Giannini founded the Bank of America when he was 60
- Col. Harlan Sanders launched KFC at age 65
- Heather Morris was 64 when she became a full-time author following her debut success with the publication of *The Tattooist of Auschwitz*

WILL YOU BE NEXT? What are you waiting for? If they can do it there's a strong likelihood you can too.

ACTION TASK! Look For Your Heroes

Gather examples of mid-life entrepreneurs who inspire you. Allow them to be your virtual mentors. How can you use their success to guide and encourage you?

WHAT YOU'VE LEARNED SO FAR

- Intensify your desire, but keep it real. Get clear about what you want to gain by being your own boss and why
- Assess any options you are considering by creating a decision-making criteria checklist
- Sometimes life 'shouts' and gives you the push you need to start your business
- Courageous action can be inspired even at what seems the

worst of times. If life is dealing you a raw hand look for opportunities that may be disguised as setbacks
- Age is no barrier to self-employment

What's Next?

Now you have a clearer idea about both your 'what' and your 'why' is, and you have awakened your desire. The next step is to work out exactly what sort of business or self-employment opportunity is right for you.

To do this there is no better place to start than to determine what sets your heart on fire.

PURSUE YOUR PASSION NOT YOUR PENSION

"The starting point of all achievement is desire."
Napoleon Hill, Author

First things first! Start from the heart.

The first and most important commandment of choosing and growing your business is to follow your passion.

Creating a successful business that you'll love is impossible without passion, enthusiasm, zest, inspiration and the deep satisfaction that comes from doing something that delivers you some kind of buzz.

Passion is a source of energy from the soul, and when you combine it with a product or service that benefits others, that's where you'll find your magic.

Kevin Roberts, former CEO of global advertising agency Saatchi and Saatchi, passionately believes that love is the way forward for business.

Meeting peoples' needs, hopes, dreams, and desires, or offering something which helps them solve problems for which they'd love a cure, is good for people and it's good for business.

"For great brands to survive, they must create Loyalty Beyond Reason," he writes in his book *Lovemarks: The Future Beyond Brands*. Roberts argues, with a ton of facts, and emotionally evocative images to support his premise, that traditional branding practices have become stultified. What's needed are customer Love affairs. "The secret," he maintains, "is the use of Mystery, Sensuality, and Intimacy."

Other experts such as Simon Sinek, author of the bestselling book *Start With Why*, and Robert Kiyosaki entrepreneur and author of the *Rich Dad, Poor Dad* books, may urge you to begin with rational, head-based logic.

I'm advocating a similar, albeit less analytical approach to begin with. But the premise is similar, to create something meaningful for yourself, and for the customers and clients you wish to attract, you must believe in what you are doing. Your business idea must matter. You must know *why* it's important—to yourself and to others.

"'*Why*' is not money or profit—these are always the results. Why does your organization exist? Why does it do the things it does? Why do customers really buy from one company or another?" challenges Sinek in his book.

I would add, *what* is its purpose? Roberts, would add, *how* can you make them fall in love with you and inspire loyalty beyond reason?

EXCERPT: MID-LIFE CAREER RESCUE (EMPLOY YOURSELF)

. . .

How to Find Your *Why*

When you discover and tap into your passion, you'll find your *why*. You'll also find a huge source of untapped potential that seems to be fearless and knows no bounds. Pursuing your passion in business is profitable on many levels.

Firstly, when you do what you love, this is most likely where your true talent lies, so you'll stand out in your field. Passion cannot be faked.

Secondly, you will be more enthusiastic about your pursuits. You will have more energy and tenacity to overcome obstacles, and more drive and determination to make things happen.

When you do what you care most about and believe in with such a passion, your work will be not something that you endure, but something that you enjoy. More importantly, work will become a vehicle for self-expression.

Thirdly, passion attracts. As multi-millionaire businesswoman Anita Roddick once said, '*We communicate with passion and passion sells.*'

Ms Roddick founded her company, The Body Shop, on one simple premise—beauty products tested on animals was cruel, barbaric, unnecessary and immoral. Millions of men and women around the world agreed.

People like to do business with people who are passionate about their products and services. When global financial services company KPMG re-branded with passion as a core theme, profitability soared. Check out my presentation on Slideshare to find out how:

http://www.slideshare.net/CassandraGaisford/passionslides-with-kpmg-slides

Hearts on Fire

The key to sound business planning begins from the inside out. First you need to determine who you are, who you want to be, and what you want to contribute to the world. In working this out, there is no better place to start than with finding out what sets you heart on fire and *why*.

Michael Jr. Comedy, a stand-up comedian and author, explains how discovering your *why* helps you develop options that enable you to live and work with purpose.

"When you know your *why*, you have options on what your *what* can be. For instance, my *why* is to inspire people to walk in purpose. My *what* is stand-up comedy. My *what* is writing books.... Another *what* that has moved me toward my *why* is a web series that we have out now called Break Time."

Check out this clip from one of Michael's most successful episodes http://bit.ly/1PnOTrH. You'll see how working with passion and purpose awakens dormant talents and enables souls to fly higher.

"When you know your *why* your *what* has more impact because you are walking toward your purpose," says Michael.

WE'LL DIVE DEEPER into discovering your life purpose in the following chapter.

SURF the Web

http://www.eofire.com: Fuel your inspiration by checking out this top-ranked business Podcast where some of the most inspiring entrepreneurs are interviewed 7-days a week. Founder and host John Lee Dumas shares his journey from frustrated employee to inspired entrepreneur via video here http://www.eofire.com/about/

DISCOVERING Your Passion

Everyone is capable of passion; some people just need help taking it out of the drawer. Look for the clues. Often this involves noticing the times you feel most energized and alive, or when you experience a surge of adrenaline through your body.

Sometimes it's the moments when time seems to fly. Perhaps it is something you love to do and would willingly do for free.

Passion is not always about love. The things that push your buttons can lead you to the things that you're most passionate about.

Working long hours, too much stress, financial strain or a whole raft of other constant pressures can soon send you drowning in a sea of negativity—killing your passion and robbing you of the energy and positivity you need to make a life-enhancing change.

If stress is taking a toll on your life you may want to check out the first book in the *Mid-Life Career Rescue* series, *The Call For Change*.

The strategies and tips in the book will help you restore the balance and get your mojo back. You'll also learn how to boost your ability to generate ideas to get unstuck. Available as a paperback and ebook from all good online stores.

If you need more help to you manage stress my book, *Stress Less. Love Life More: How to Stop Worrying, Reduce Anxiety, Eliminate Negative Thinking and Find Happiness*, available as a paperback and eBook will help.

Action Task! Find Your Passion

Real passion is more than a fad or a fleeting enthusiasm. It can't be turned on and off like a light switch. Answering the following questions will help you begin to clarify the things you are most passionate about:

1. **When does time seem to fly?** When was the last time you felt really excited, or deeply absorbed in, or obsessed by

something? What were you doing? Who were you with? What clues did you notice?
2. **What do you care deeply or strongly about?** Discovering all the things that you believe in is not always easy. Look for the clues to your deep beliefs by catching the times you use words such as 'should' or 'must.'
3. **What do you value?** What do you need to experience, feel, or be doing to feel deeply fulfilled?
4. **What pushes your buttons or makes you angry?** How could you use your anger constructively to bring about change?
5. **Which skills and talents come most easily or naturally to you?** Which skills do you love using? What skills do you look forward to using? What gives you such a buzz or a huge sense of personal satisfaction that you'd keep doing it even if you weren't paid?
6. **What inspires you?** To be inspired is to be in spirit. What bewitches and enthralls you so much that you lose all track of time? What makes your soul sing? What floats your boat? What things, situations, people, events etc. fill you with feelings of inspiration? List all your obsessions and the things that interest you deeply. If you're struggling to identify your interests and inspirations, you'll find some handy prompts in the next chapter.
7. **Keep a passion journal.** My passion is passion—to help others live and work with passion and to bring about positive change in the world. If you're not sure what you are passionate about, creating a passion journal is one simple but powerful technique to help achieve clarity. Your passion journal is where manifesting your preferred future really happens. I've been keeping a passion journal for years and so many things I've visualized and affirmed on the pages, are now my living realities—personally and professionally.

Love Is Where The Magic Is

Love is where the magic is. When you love what you do with such a passion you'd do it for free this is your path with heart. You've heard the saying, 'when you do what you love, you'll never work again.' It's true. Work doesn't feel like a slog, it feels energizing.

As Annie Featherston, writing as Sophia James, shared in the second book on the *Mid-Life Career Rescue* series, *What Makes You Happy*, "When you combine your favorite skills with doing something you completely and utterly love, you come home to your True Self and find your place of bliss. The result? Contentment—and more often than not, producing something highly marketable."

Passion in Business

A good way to find your own passion and identify ways to turn it into a fulfilling self-employment opportunity is to look for examples of others who have started businesses they are passionate about.

Here are just a few of many examples:

A passion for bugs! Brian Clifford is passionate about helping people and bugs. He has combined his passion into a successful business as a pest controller.

"All the rats, all the maggots, all the cockroaches all over the place, these are the things that I love doing,' he says. His business motto is, 'If it bugs you, I'll kill it!"

Check out his business here >> www.borercontrolwellington.co.nz

A passion for bones! John Holley has turned his passion for bones into a business, Skulls Down Under, selling skeletons to museums all over the world.

Check out his business here >> www.skullsdownunder.co.nz

. . .

A PASSION FOR MAORI FOOD. Charles Royal's passion for finding a way to incorporate traditional Maori foods into modern dishes led him to start his own business—Kinaki Wild Herbs.

"I had learned a lot about the bush during my time in the army and have taken that knowledge through the years, developing food tours and cooking classes using what we gather from the wild. I love organics and making something out of nothing, but you have to know what you are looking for," says Royal. Air New Zealand now serves pikopiko and horopito in its First and Business Classes.

Check out his business here >> www.maorifood.com

SUCCESS STORY: A LOVE OF GOOD FOOD

"Passion is Everything—If You Don't Have It You Will Not Succeed"

A love of good food and a lifelong dream to open their passion-driven business in London fueled Wellington restauranteurs Vivienne Haymans and Ashley Sumners' move to the UK.

> "We both felt we had gone as far as we could with our business in New Zealand and wanted to move further afield," says Vivienne.

> "I came here for a three-month holiday, secretly wanting to stay longer and build a business overseas. On arriving I discovered that London seriously needed a restaurant like our Sugar Club in Wellington. There was nowhere in London doing anything like it. I called Ash and a year later he also moved to London after selling our Wellington restaurant."

> They relocated the restaurant to Notting Hill in 1995, then to Soho in 1998, winning the Time Out "Best Modern British Restaurant" award in 1996 and "Best Central London Restaurant" award in 1999, along with several Evening Standard Eros awards.

Since then they have expanded and diversified their restaurant business, opening a chain of modern *traiteurs* (Italian-style delicatessens) that offer delicious, easy-to-prepare hand-made meals and great New Zealand coffee.

The first of these is called The Grocer on Elgin, situated in the heart of Notting Hill. Vivienne designed all three restaurants and 'The Grocer On' stores.

Like many people following their passion, Vivienne and Ash faced significant barriers before finally making it big.

"It took Ash and I seven years to fulfill our dream of opening The Sugar Club in London. When we first arrived there were huge premiums being asked for restaurant sites.

Then, with the early 90s recession they were giving restaurants away but, like now, the banks were not lending. We had no property assets at the time, limited funds, a reference from our NZ lawyer, accountant and bank manager and a handful of NZ press clippings. The banks wanted property assets and UK business records. No less."

Just when it looked like the obstacles were insurmountable, their passion for great food and design, the quality of the produce, and the integrity of its production, produced lucky fruit.

"We were offered a site by a landlord that we had had dealings with in the past. He liked what we did and gave us the lease. We developed the old Singapore Pandang into the Notting Hill Sugar Club. I borrowed an extra £5000 from my mum and paid her back in a month. It was an instant success and well worth the long wait."

Vivienne says that following their passion is an important ingredient in their success.

"Passion is everything—if you don't have it you will not succeed. It is hard work; your passion will pull you through the seriously bad times, which will always occur."

Hot Tip! Gathering your own examples of passionate people and businesses is a great way to build confidence and generate your own business ideas.

Here are some things that other people who are self-employed are passionate about:

- **Creating Businesses**—Entrepreneurs Melissa Clarke Reynolds and Eric Watson
- **Airports**—Graham is an airport designer
- **Boats**—Bill Day runs a specialist maritime service business
- **Beauty**—Joy Gaisford, Designer
- **Food**—Ruth Pretty, Caterer and food writer
- **Astronomy**—Richard Hall, Stonehenge Aotearoa
- **Design**—Luke Pierson, runs a web design business
- **Rocks**—Carl created Carlucciland—a rock-themed amusement park
- **Passion**—Cassandra Gaisford helping people work and live their passion!

Here are some things that some businesses are passionate about:

- **Animal Welfare and Human Rights**—The Body Shop
- **Technology**—Microsoft, Apple
- **Helping people**—Worklife Solutions, Venus Network
- **Equality**—The EEO Trust, and the Johnstone Group
- **The Environment**—The Conservation Department
- **Honey**—The Honey Hive
- **Chocolate**—Chocaholic
- **Pampering Others**—East Day Spa

Tune In To Your Body Barometer

What pushes your buttons or makes you angry? Having my manager threaten to 'smash my head in,' and working with others who were bullies and tyrants, the relentless pursuit of profit at the expense of caring for people, and numerous work restructurings, motivated me to gain my independence.

That and getting shingles—something I wrote about in my first books, *The Call for Change*, and also *What Makes You Happy*.

Shingles was definitely my body barometer sending me a red alert! As was seeing my colleagues suffer heart attacks.

As Neale Walsch, the author of *Conversations with God*, says, "Judge not about which you feel passionate. Simply notice it, then see if it serves you, given who and what you wish to be."

So, as I've mentioned earlier, rather than become bitter, I thought how could I use my anger constructively to bring about change?

I decided I wanted to help people find jobs that made them happy, and I wanted to help victims of workplace bullying. That was my *why* and my *what*.

Stepping Stones to Success

I started a career counseling business for an established workplace counseling organization before going out on my own.

Working as an employee first gave me the confidence to fly free. I became more motivated when the CEO changed and the new boss tried to manage me. Increasingly, the job began to frustrate me.

It lacked challenge, my salary was capped, and I was finding it increasingly difficult to balance childcare. The final clincher however was when I did the math.

I worked out my hourly rate as a full-time salaried employee, versus what they charged me out per hour, and how much business I was bringing in for them, and came to the conclusion they were buying my skills, but they weren't paying me enough. I could work less and earn and achieve more if I employed myself. I started to feel excited!

ACTION TASK! Tune into Your Body Barometer

Notice the times you feel strong emotions. These could be annoyance, irritation and anger. Or they could be a sense of excitement, a state of arousal, a feeling of limitless energy, a burning desire, a strong gut feeling, a feeling of contentment or determination. Notice these feelings and record them in your passion journal.

Go deeper. Ask, "How could I make a living from my passion?" or "How do others make a living from things that excite or motivate me?"

Explore possibilities. Even a simple Google search, or generating ideas with others could get you started down the right path.

** FREE BONUS **

If you haven't downloaded the free copy of the Passion Workbook, download it here >>http://worklifesolutions.leadpages.co/free-find-your-passion-workbook.

WHAT YOU'VE LEARNED SO FAR

- Passion is energy. It is emotion, zest, intensity, enthusiasm and excitement. Passion is love
- Creating more love in the world is the way forward for business. Meeting peoples' needs, hopes, dreams and desires, or offering something which helps them solve problems for which they'd love a cure, is good for people and its good for business
- Do what moves you. Pursuing your passion, not your

WHAT YOU'VE LEARNED SO FAR

- pension, can be a liberating and clarifying catalyst to your true calling and the business you were born to create
- A healthy obsession can lead to many things. Not only will your passion lead you to your path with heart, it will also help fuel the fires of determination, courage and self-belief. You'll be fully alive, stand out from the crowd and gain a competitive edge
- If you don't know where to look, passion can be difficult to find. Tune into your body barometer and notice the times when you feel most alive, inspired or fulfilled
- Start a passion journal—keep track of the times when you notice clues to your passion, such as a feeling of inspiration or any of the other signs discussed in this chapter. Record these moments so that they don't get lost or forgotten
- Adding quotes, pictures or any other insights will really make your journal come alive. Gain greater awareness of what drives your passion by asking yourself, "Why am I passionate about this?" Look for the themes and patterns that build up over time
- Keep your passion alive by updating your journal and referring to it regularly. Actively look for examples of people who have made the things you are passionate about into a rewarding business

What's Next?

In the next chapter you'll discover how joyous and exciting work and life is when you're working with a higher purpose.

Did you enjoy this excerpt?

Grab The Ultimate Guide to Freedom

Mid-Life Career Rescue: Employ Yourself

Start a business on the side while holding down your job. Or take the leap to self-employed bliss. Choose and grow your own business with confidence. This handy resource will show you how.

Available in print and eBook.

DID YOU ENJOY THIS EXCERPT?

If you need more help and a step-by-step guide to becoming your own boss my book, *Employ Yourself*, available as a paperback and eBook from all good online books stores will help.

To fuel the flames of inspiration to help you create a passion and purpose inspired business, The Passion-Driven Business Planning Journal: The Effortless Path to Manifesting Your Business and Career Goals, available as a paperback and eBbook will help.

Or you may prefer to take my online course, and watch inspirational and practical videos and other strategies to help you to fulfil your potential—https://the-coaching-lab.teachable.com/p/follow-your-passion-and-purpose-to-prosperity.

AFTERWORD

I hope you have found a few useful tips in this book to help you control anxiety, conquer stress and fuel greater resilience. Mastering the ability to slay toxic stress dragons lies at the heart of your mental, emotional, spiritual, and physical well-being.

I always believe that I should practice what I preach and so you can be sure that many of the strategies and techniques I have shared with you are ones I have put into practice myself. Writing this book is a case in point. It really was a case of putting all that I knew into practice—once again.

This book is a labor of love, passion, and purpose. One that had its seeds in the culmination and intersection of my talents, my interests, my motivations, and external drivers. Life kept telling me that this was a book I not only wanted to write, but was called to write.

Requests from my readers and also from clients provided a compelling reminder to crack on and finish this book.

External factors also spurred my motivation, like juggling work, running multiple businesses, supporting my partner through family

AFTERWORD

dramas—and then, as if I wasn't "stressed" enough, a toxic, narcissistic employer stole what little peace of mind I had managed to salvage.

So, yes—life is stressful. Sometimes exceedingly stressful. There's so much and so many people lining up to feed your anxiety—if you let them. I've discovered first-hand just how essential it is to build resilience ahead of time. I hope you have, too.

I've also learned to revalue the spiritually-motivating power of living to a purpose and strengthened my intuitive powers in the process.

I've been inspired by the American singer, Meatloaf. His mission to find a producer for his album *Bat Out of Hell* is such an inspirational story about passion, grit, perseverance, failure, and ultimate success.

Plus, I've followed one of my muses, Richard Branson, whose wise words, "If it's not fun I'm not doing it," have reminded me to always work with joy.

Follow Your Joy

What is my joy? Well, I have several, but one of the most important is that by writing this book I have helped you gain the clarity, confidence, courage and inspiration to live a happy, healthy life and to follow your dreams.

I dream that you, and those you love, can be truly happy, and that your happiness will spread the seeds of joy amongst all you meet.

I dream that one day the current research that states that less than 80% of people are suffering from anxiety will be surpassed by new data showing that over 80% of people are happy at work and in life.

Is this really dreaming? Decide for yourself. Perhaps, this book will help you to turn your dreams of a happy working life into a fulfilling reality.

Thank you for allowing me to go on this journey with you. Stay optimistic—you can handle anything that comes your way.

Passionately and happily yours,

Cassandra

P.S. What feeds your spirit?

I feel passionately about spiritually approaches to healing. As one of my clients, a 10-year-old boy I taught to meditate as part of his anxiety, and anger cure, said to me,

"Thanks for meditating with me. It was like being on another planet."

In response to this feedback, I wrote a second book in the *Anxiety Rescue* series called, *Love Your Soul*.

In *Love Your Soul*, I'll help you clarify what you need to feel happy, enriched with purpose, and to be fulfilled. Plus we'll dive deeper into discovering your vein of gold—the strengths, gifts and natural talents you have to give the world.

If you'd like to be the first to know when this and other books become available, sign up for my newsletter and receive free giveaways, sneak peeks into new books and helpful tips and strategies to live life more passionately.

FOLLOW YOUR PASSION TO PROSPERITY ONLINE COURSE

If you need more help to find and live your life purpose you may prefer to take my online course, and watch inspirational and practical videos and other strategies to help you to fulfill your potential.

Follow your passion and purpose to prosperity—online coaching program

Easily discover your passion and purpose, overcoming barriers to success, and create a job or business you love with my self-paced online course.

Gain unlimited lifetime access to this course, for as long as you like—across any and all devices you own. Be supported with practical, inspirational, easy-to-access strategies to achieve your dreams.

To start achieving outstanding personal and professional results with absolute certainty and excitement. **Click here to enroll or find out more—** https://the-coaching-lab.teachable.com/p/follow-your-passion-and-purpose-to-prosperity

FREE WORKBOOK!

The Passion Journal: The Effortless Path to Manifesting Your Love, Life, and Career Goals

Thank you for your interest in my new book.
To show my appreciation, I'm excited to be giving you another book for FREE!

Download the free *Passion Journal Workbook* here>>https://dl.bookfunnel.com/aepj97k2n1

I hope you enjoy it—it's dedicated to helping you live and work with passion, resilience and joy.

You'll also be subscribed to my newsletter and receive free giveaways, insights into my writing life, new release advance alerts and inspirational tips to help you live and work with passion, joy, and prosperity. Opt out at anytime.

FURTHER RESOURCES

SURF THE NET

www.bornthisway.foundation

Founded by Lady Gaga to empower youth, inspire bravery and encourage kindness. Offers inspiration, support, and research to promote mental health.

Mathew Johnstone has a wide range of books and resources on mental wellness and mindfulness: www.matthewjohnstone.com.au

Brad Yates shares a wonderful way to self-help your way through anxiety to self-love in his YouTube videos. You can check it one of them here—https://youtu.be/K6kq9N9Yp6E

www.whatthebleep.com—a powerful and inspiring site emphasizing quantum physics and the transformational power of thought.

www.heartmath.org—comprehensive information and tools help you access your intuitive insight and heart-based knowledge. Validated and supported by science-based research. Check out the additional information about your heart-brain.

Join polymath Tim Ferris and learn from his interesting and informative guests on The Tim Ferris Show http://fourhourworkweek.com/podcast/.

Listen to podcasts which inspire you to become the best version of your writing self—*Joanna Penn's podcast* is very helpful for "authorpreneurs" http://www.thecreativepenn.com/podcasts. I also love Neil Patel's podcast for savvy marketing strategies http://neilpatel.com/podcast.

Experience the transformative power of hypnosis. One of my favorite hypnosis sites is the UK-based Uncommon Knowledge. On their website http://www.hypnosisdownloads.com you'll find a range of self-hypnosis mp3 audios, including The Millionaire Mindset program.

Celebrity hypnotherapist and author Marissa Peer is another favorite source of subconscious reprogramming and liberation—www.marisapeer.com.

What beliefs are holding you back? Check out Peer's Youtube clip "How To Teach Your Mind That Everything Is Available To You" here —https://www.youtube.com/watch?v=IKeaAbM2kJg

Enjoy James Clear's fabulous blog content and receive further self-improvement tips based on proven scientific research: http://jamesclear.com/articles

Tim Ferriss recommends a couple of apps for those wanting some help getting started with meditation—Headspace (www.headspace.com) or Calm (www.calm.com).

National Geographic: The Science of Stress: Portrait of a killer

https://www.youtube.com/watch?v=ZyBsy5SQxqU

Effects of Stress on Your Body

https://www.youtube.com/watch?v=1p6EeYwp1O4

Mindfulness training

Wellington-based Peter Fernando offers an introductory guided meditation which you can take further. He also meets with individuals and groups in Wellington for philosophical talks on mindfulness and Buddhism. Very enjoyable and great for the soul.

http://www.monthofmindfulness.info

Guided meditations

www.calm.com

Free app with guided meditations

http://eocinstitute.org/meditation/emotional-benefits-of-meditation/

Includes a comprehensive list of the benefits of meditation.

Career Guidance Sites:

www.aarp.org/work - information and tools to help you stay current and connected with what's hot and what's not in today's workplace.

www.lifereimagined.org - loads of inspiration and practical tips to help you maximize your interests and expertise, personalized and interactive.

www.whatthebleep.com – a powerful and inspiring site emphasizing quantum physics and the transformational power of thought.

www.personalitytype.com—created by the authors of *Do What You Are: Discover the Perfect Career for You through the Secrets of Personality Type*. This site focuses on expanding your awareness of your own type and that of others—including children and partners. This site also contains many useful links.

FURTHER RESOURCES

BOOKS

Repurpose trauma with Azita Nahai, *Trauma to Dharma: Transform Your Pain into Purpose*

Treatment of Complex Trauma: A Sequenced, Relationship-Based Approach by Christine Courtois and Julian Ford

Journey Through Trauma: A Trail Guide to the 5-Phase Cycle of Healing Repeated Trauma by Gretchen Schmelzer, PhD

The Complex PTSD Workbook: A Mind-Body Approach to Regaining Emotional Control and Becoming Whole by Arielle Schwartz, PhD

The Body Keeps Score: Brain, Mind, And Body In The Healing Of Trauma by Bessel van der Kolk

Struggling in an extroverted world? Introverts are enjoying a renaissance, fueled in part by Susan Cain's terrific bestseller, *Quiet: The Power of Introverts in a World That Can't Stop Talking.*

Roll up your sleeves and bring out the big guns to win your creative battle with *The War of Art* by Steven Pressfield.

Power up with a new personality—read Breaking the Habit of Being Yourself: How to Lose Your Mind and Create a New One by Dr. Joe Dispenza.

Unleash the power of your mind by reading *You Are the Placebo: Making Your Mind Matter,* by Dr. Joe Dispenza.

Manifest your prosperity with Rhonda Byrne in her popular book, *The Secret.*

Ensure you don't starve by reading Jeff Goins collated wisdom in *Real Artists Don't Starve: Timeless Strategies for Thriving in the New Creative Age.*

FURTHER RESOURCES

Fortify your faith with Julia Cameron's book, *Faith and Will*.

How to Survive and Thrive in Any Life Crisis, Dr. Al Siebert

Thrive: The Third Metric to Redefining Success and Creating a Happier Life, Arianna Huffington

(This book has great content throughout and some excellent resources listed in the back.)

The Power of Now: A Guide to Spiritual Enlightenment, Eckhart Tolle

The Book of Joy, The Dalai Lama and Archbishop Desmond Tutu

The Sleep Revolution: Transforming Your Life One Night at a Time, Arianna Huffington

Quiet the Mind: An Illustrated Guide on How to Meditate, Mathew Johnstone

Comfortable with Uncertainty: 108 Teachings on Cultivating Fearlessness and Compassion, Pema Chodron

Power vs. Force: The Hidden Determinants of Human Behavior, David R. Hawkins

Learn how to live an inspired life with Tarot cards and other oracles. Read Jessa Crispin's book, *The Creative Tarot: A Modern Guide to an Inspired Life*.

Check out all of Collette-Baron-Reid's books, including: *Uncharted: The Journey Through Uncertainty to Infinite Possibility* and *Messages from Spirit: The Extraordinary Power of Oracles, Omens, and Signs*.

PLEASE LEAVE A REVIEW

Word of mouth is the most powerful marketing force in the universe. If you found this book useful, I'd appreciate you rating this book and leaving a review. You don't have to say much—just a few words about how the book helped you learn something new or made you feel.

"Your books are a fantastic resource and until now I never even thought to write a review. Going forward I will be reviewing more books. So many great ones out there and I want to support the amazing people that write them."

Great reviews help people find good books.

Thank you so much! I appreciate you!

PS: If you enjoyed this book, do me a small favour to help spread the word about it and share on Facebook, Twitter and other social networks.

BLOSSOM

"Blossom into your dharma, that which you are meant to become. It is the music you are playing out in the world."

~ Pam Gregory

ALSO BY CASSANDRA GAISFORD

Transformational Super Kids:

The Little Princess
The Little Princess Can Fly
I Have to Grow
The Boy Who Cried

Mid-Life Career Rescue:

The Call for Change
What Makes You Happy
Employ Yourself
Job Search Strategies That Work
3 Book Box Set: The Call for Change, What Makes You Happy, Employ Yourself
4 Book Box Set: The Call for Change, What Makes You Happy, Employ Yourself, Job Search Strategies That Work

Career Change:

ALSO BY CASSANDRA GAISFORD

Career Change 2020 5 Book-Bundle Box Set

Master Life Coach:

Leonardo da Vinci: Life Coach
Coco Chanel: Life Coach

The Art of Living:

How to Find Your Passion and Purpose
How to Find Your Passion and Purpose Companion Workbook
Career Rescue: The Art and Science of Reinventing Your Career and Life
Boost Your Self-Esteem and Confidence
Anxiety Rescue
No! Why 'No' is the New 'Yes'
How to Find Your Joy and Purpose
How to Find Your Joy and Purpose Companion Workbook

The Art of Success:

Leonardo da Vinci
Coco Chanel

Journaling Prompts Series:

The Passion Journal
The Passion-Driven Business Planning Journal
How to Find Your Passion and Purpose 2 Book-Bundle Box Set

Health & Happiness:

The Happy, Healthy Artist
Stress Less. Love Life More
Bounce: Overcoming Adversity, Building Resilience and Finding Joy
Bounce Companion Workbook

ALSO BY CASSANDRA GAISFORD

Mindful Sobriety:

Mind Your Drink: The Surprising Joy of Sobriety
Mind Over Mojitos: How Moderating Your Drinking Can Change Your Life: Easy Recipes for Happier Hours & a Joy-Filled Life
Your Beautiful Brain: Control Alcohol and Love Life More

Happy Sobriety:

Happy Sobriety: Non-Alcoholic Guilt-Free Drinks You'll Love
The Sobriety Journal
Happy Sobriety Two Book Bundle-Box Set: Alcohol and Guilt-Free Drinks You'll Love & *The Sobriety Journal*

Money Manifestation:

Financial Rescue: The Total Money Makeover: Create Wealth, Reduce Debt & Gain Freedom

The Prosperous Author:

Developing a Millionaire Mindset
Productivity Hacks: Do Less & Make More
Two Book Bundle-Box Set (Books 1-2)

Miracle Mindset:

Change Your Mindset: Millionaire Mindset Makeover: The Power of Purpose, Passion, & Perseverance

Non-Fiction:

Where is Salvator Mundi?

More of Cassandra's practical and inspiring workbooks on a range of

ALSO BY CASSANDRA GAISFORD

career and life-enhancing topics are on her website (www.cassandragaisford.com) and her author page at all good online bookstores.

ABOUT THE AUTHOR

CASSANDRA GAISFORD is best known as *The Queen of Uplifting Inspiration*.

A former holistic therapist, award-winning artist, and #1 bestselling author. A corporate escapee, she now lives and works from her idyllic lifestyle property overlooking the Bay of Islands in New Zealand.

Cassandra's unique blend of business experience and qualifications (BCA, Dip Psych.), creative skills, and wellness and holistic training (Dip Counselling, Reiki Master Teacher) blends pragmatism and commercial savvy with rare and unique insight and out-of-the-box-thinking for anyone wanting to achieve an extraordinary life.

STAY IN TOUCH

Become a fan and Continue To Be Supported, Encouraged, and Inspired

Subscribe to my newsletter and follow me on BookBub (https://www.bookbub.com/profile/cassandra-gaisford) and be the first to know about my new releases and giveaways

www.cassandragaisford.com
www.facebook.com/cassandra.gaisford
www.instagram.com/cassandragaisford
www.youtube.com/cassandragaisfordnz
www.pinterest.com/cassandraNZ
www.linkedin.com/in/cassandragaisford
www.twitter.com/cassandraNZ

And please, do check out some of my videos where I share strategies and tips to stress less and love life more—http://www.youtube.com/cassandragaisfordnz

I invite you to share your stories and experiences in our Career Rescue

STAY IN TOUCH

Community. We'd love to hear from you! To join, visit https://www.facebook.com/Career_Rescue

BLOG

Subscribe and be inspired by regular posts to help you increase your wellness, follow your bliss, slay self-doubt, and sustain healthy habits.

Learn more about how to achieve happiness and success at work and life by visiting my blog:

www.cassandragaisford.com/archives

SPEAKING EVENTS

Cassandra is available internationally for speaking events aimed at wellness strategies, motivation, inspiration and as a keynote speaker.

She has an enthusiastic, humorous and passionate style of delivery and is celebrated for her ability to motivate, inspire and enlighten.

For information navigate to www.cassandragaisford.com/contact/speaking

To ask Cassandra to come and speak at your workplace or conference, contact: cassandra@cassandragaisford.com

NEWSLETTERS

For inspiring tools and helpful tips subscribe to Cassandra's free newsletters here:
http://www.cassandragaisford.com

Sign up now and receive a free eBook to help you find your passion and purpose!
http://eepurl.com/bEArfT

ACKNOWLEDGMENTS

This book (and my new life) was made possible by the amazing generosity, open heartedness, and wonderful friendship of so many people. Thank you!

To all the amazingly interesting clients who have allowed me to help them over the years, and to the wonderful people who read my books and wrote to me with their stories of reinvention—thank you. Your feedback, deep sharing, requests for help, and inspired, courageous action continues to inspire me.

I'm also grateful to the Health Editor of *Marie Claire* magazine whom, after she had accepted a short article, said I had the bones of a good book and should write it.

My thanks also to my terrific friends and supporters. And, of course, I can never say thank you enough to my family, particularly my parents and grandparents, who have instilled me with such tremendous values and life skills.

My daughter, Hannah—I wish for you everything that your heart desires. Without you, I doubt I would ever have accomplished all the things I have in my life.

Thank you.

COPYRIGHT

Copyright © 2019 Cassandra Gaisford
Published by Blue Giraffe Publishing 2019

Blue Giraffe Publishing is a division of Worklife Solutions Ltd.

Cover Design by Steven Novak

All rights reserved. No part of this publication may be reproduced, distributed, or transmitted in any form or by any means, including photocopying, recording, or other electronic or mechanical methods, without the prior written permission of the author or publisher, except in the case of brief quotations embodied in reviews and certain other non-commercial uses permitted by copyright law.

Neither the publisher nor the author are engaged in rendering professional advice or services to the individual reader. The ideas, procedures, and suggestions contained in this book are not intended as a substitute for psychotherapy, counseling, or consulting with your physician.

The intent of the author is only to offer information of a general

COPYRIGHT

nature to help you in your quest for emotional, physical, and spiritual well-being.

Any use of information in this book is at the reader's discretion and risk. Neither the author nor the publisher can be held responsible for any loss, claim or damage arising out of the use, or misuse, of the suggestions made, the failure to take medical advice or for any material on third party websites.

ISBN PRINT: 978-0-9951137-7-0

ISBN EBOOK: 978-0-9951137-7-0

ISBN HARDCOVER: 978-1-99-002001-8

First Edition